The Year of Talkii

The plants and fairies talk in their own words

words

SARAH RAJKOTWALA

The Year of Talking to Plants: The Plants and Fairies Talk in Their Own Words

Sarah Rajkotwala

Published by Sarah Rajkotwala, 2017.

THE YEAR OF TALKING TO PLANTS: THE PLANTS AND FAIRIES TALK IN THEIR OWN WORDS

First edition. May 20, 2017.

Copyright © 2017 Sarah Rajkotwala.

ISBN: 979-8223822745

Written by Sarah Rajkotwala.

Also by Sarah Rajkotwala

The Year of Talking to Plants: The Plants and Fairies Talk in Their Own Words

Fairy Sparkles: My Journey With Angels, Fairies, Nature and Spiritual Enlightenment. One Woman's Adventure Into Falling In Love With Life

Conversations With My Vegetable Garden: Growing Vegetables With The Help Of The Vegetable Garden Fairies

Watch for more at https://petalsandbuds.wordpress.com/.

Table of Contents

To my family,

My guides and angels, Mother Earth and all the plants & fairies of the world, with love.

First published in 2017 by Sarah Rajkotwala
Website – http://petalsandbuds@wordpress.com
First edition

 A catalogue record for this book is available from the National Library of Australia

The front cover design is designed by R L Sather from Self Pub Book Covers.com

Preface

If you thought there was more to your garden than meets the eye, a spiritual element, then read on. This is the record of my very first year of talking to the plants in my garden. It is an in-depth discussion with the plants and as I was later to find out their accompanying fairies. We discuss the fairies' significance and importance in all of our lives, the wellbeing of our gardens and the planet as a whole.

Here is the story I wrote as I first learned to converse with the plants. Some of the insights from the plants are amazing, others inspirational and the rest just plain useful. As I conversed, I wrote down exactly what they told me word for word, so I could make an accurate record of what I heard.

What you will read is plants talking in their own words, as I addressed them plant by plant, like a kind of spiritual reporter. I asked questions all around the issue of just what is a fairy and what is their role in our gardens?

I tried to get to the bottom of what plants do, in a spiritual and physical way for humankind. I was fascinated by the idea of fairies going around our gardens, unseen by most of us. So as I gradually learned more about them, I was not disappointed with their responses.

In this book I am combining the everyday experience of gardening with the seemingly other-worldly experience of being able to communicate with the plants telepathically. Although, as I soon found out there are many reasons why it is beneficial that people are aware of the world that the plants exist in and how to cooperate with the fairy realm. Fairies surround us every day, they are already a part of our lives whether we know it or not. We might as well get to know them. Communicating with plants will provide our society with many insights and blessings. As you start to believe in them you will begin to perceive and multiply their blessings for yourself.

Introduction

I have been a keen gardener for many years, spending every spare moment happily playing and aiming to create a beautiful oasis out of every garden I resided in. Gardening and learning about plants has been an engrossing and creative passion all of my adult life. Throughout this time, I have learnt a great deal of conventional knowledge about gardening. At one stage I even had my own plant nursery where I was surrounded by plants on a daily basis. Some of my happiest times have been spent in my various gardens amongst the plants and animals, lovingly tending and enjoying them. Always aiming to make each garden I have lived in a little more beautiful as each year passes, hoping to create my own little heaven on earth. As though my one little garden had the power to change all with its beauty and love, perhaps on some level it does.

The Beginning of My Garden Adventure

Around the age of fourteen I helped my mother plant a punnet of lobelias around the base of some gigantic old rose bushes and then without warning this little act ignited a passion for all things gardening. The very possibility that I could plant these tiny little objects and they would grow into a mass of azure blue flowers beneath the roses, making a beautiful garden picture I found very exciting. I have been a passionate gardener ever since, with a particular love for profuse cottage gardens that bloom with freedom, abundance and joy. At every home that I resided in from that time on I have planted a wild plant-filled oasis, be it a rented bed-sit, a suburban plot or a large rambling country garden. Each garden was a little more ambitious than the last, my horticultural ambitions grew proportionately with the size of each new gardening space. I adore every aspect of gardening; I love the challenge of turning a barren piece of land into a verdant paradise.

My Spiritual Quest

Coinciding with my gradual learning about all things gardening I was also following a passion for the spiritual side of life. It would be true to say these are my two main passions, gardening and spiritual enlightenment. I enjoyed and pursued both of these interests separately for many years. I suppose it was inevitable that I was to find a link (or at least the Universe did) between these two passions. I did not look for a link beyond knowing that nature was indeed God's magnificent work of beauty and love, there to be experienced with joy and reverence. Although I always somehow believed in fairies and that the plants were conscious in some way.

It was around my fortieth year that I was to find that apart from being a nurseryperson and a passionate gardener, I was able to do one more thing with plants. I found out almost by accident, (although I don't really believe in accidents or coincidences as such). I believe that everything happens for a reason and that the whole world and Universe is conscious and intelligent. Synchronicity and coincidences are manufactured by the Universe, our higher-selves, guides and angels for our benefit, growth and ultimate happiness.

THE YEAR OF TALKING TO PLANTS: THE PLANTS AND FAIRIES TALK IN THEIR OWN WORDS

One day I was lying on an energy healers table for my first session. Virtually the first thing she said to me was that I meditated and had a ritual to how I do it (she was also psychic). This was true I meditate on a regular basis and had a ritual of how I went about it. She then said, 'There is another thing you can do too', mysteriously she left it at that and that was all that was said on the subject. That was it, but there was something enigmatic about those words that I just had to get to the bottom of. What sort of thing could I do? Was it to do with keeping myself centered and calm like yoga? The healer said it was something to do with plants. It was not until later that I found out what the spiritual thing that I could do was. I could talk to plants!

Talking to Plants

I was amazed. It wasn't that plants could talk; I already somehow instinctively knew this. It was that I didn't know I could talk to them! How could I have lived my whole life around plants and had no inkling of what I could do?

Interestingly a few years earlier I read in a book that you could communicate to plants if you showed genuine love and concern for them and communicated to them via love. So I promptly went outside and beamed some love at a plant, but nothing, no word of communication, no sign in response. I thought it must have been a particular skill that I didn't have. So I forgot about it and got on with life. The interesting thing about this was that I had such a desire to communicate with plants. The absolutely amazing thing is if, then and there, I had indeed addressed the plant either talked to it mentally or out-loud, it probably would have talked back to me! There was no need to beam love at them, the plants already knew I loved them anyway! Plants respond to my words with their words, via mental telepathy.

Mental Telepathy

Only crazy people talk to plants, right? Wrong! But I didn't talk to them seriously in all my years of gardening and working very closely with them. Despite occasionally coming across an 'eccentric' customer in my plant nursery saying they talked to their plants and believed that it seemed to do them some good. If I did accidentally talk to them and got a mental response from them, I probably would have disregarded it anyway, putting it down to an over-fertile imagination. However, I have since learned that with mental telepathy (the main way I communicate with them) and with many other ways of getting psychic and intuitive messages, your imagination is the place where these messages are received. That is why telepathic thoughts seem to talk to you using your own vocabulary and familiar mind-pictures, within your own mind because it is your own vocabulary and collections of known images, words and concepts that are used, by transferring their thoughts to you. That is how telepathy works.

The Mistaken Answer

Also remarkably a few years prior to this, I accidentally spoke out loud to a plant. I have a collection of heritage rose plants in my rose garden and sometimes I received varieties that had been mis-labelled, not what I bought them as. For a few seasons I was trying to narrow down what variety this particular rose bush was, it looked like an Alba rose that flowered once a year. One day on inspecting it I said out loud "Who are you?" Then quick as a wink, in my mind I got a response, "Amelia". I knew this was an answer to my question. I promptly rushed inside to consult my rose books and yes this was exactly what my rose looked like; the alba rose 'Amelia'! The answer to my question was spot-on. I knew I received the correct information psychically, but misattributed the source. I thought it was information from my spirit guides, thinking wow I must have a rose expert in spirit giving me some advice! Ha! So there you go, I was given big heavy clues that I could talk to plants and still didn't comprehend that I could. Yes, I believed that I could get psychic information from an invisible spirit guide, but not the plants themselves! However, I was one step away from my surprise discovery.

My First Try

So after finding out I could talk to plants from the healer, that week I went home to see if I could talk to plants. Incredibly when I addressed a plant the first time, it seemed to give a response back, via words that were put in my mind, a sort of mental telepathy. It still didn't seem that I was really talking to plants, it seemed like I was having a conversation with myself, making it all up. I looked at a small groundcover and asked how it was; it said 'I'm thirsty' (The whole garden was in need of water; it was mid-summer). Somehow deep down I knew that I was truly communicating with the plant. To any normal person this is indeed a strange skill to have but to me, who has spent my whole life being blissfully engrossed with plants, this information was absolutely amazing. I could have used this years ago to my garden's and my advantage. Wow!

The Dialogue with the Plants Throughout this Book

Throughout this book I have interspersed interviews I have given with individual plants as I walked around my garden, and later on when I was introduced to a fairy.

Their answers have been surprising and sometimes profound, as have indeed all my communications with the plant world. I rather thought that plants might talk in a simplistic way like 'me hungry, me thirsty', but I was well off the mark! The sophisticated, learned and loving conversations I have had with them were a delightful surprise. We could all learn a thing or two about peace, love, and joy from our leafy friends.

The dialogue in fancy script at the beginning of the chapters and scattered throughout the text is my own writing (not fairy quotes, with two exceptions which I have noted), it is of a spiritual and joyful nature, written to enhance your reading experience.

Chapter 1
Verification

Winter in my garden is like spring in a raincoat.

I have had to consciously remember to talk to my plants which is part of the reason I am writing this book. After forty years of not talking to the plants and flowers around me, I have to make the effort to say something to them. It is as if all the game-plan has changed and I am just getting used to the new rules.

It is not as though I can hear them talking, it is a subtle psychic skill. Psychic awareness can be quiet and ephemeral, so to talk in my mind or out loud to the plants takes conscious effort. I do not yet know whether everyone can communicate as easily as I can or if even a certain percentage of the population can but doesn't know it yet, this will take more enquiry. Physic awareness is a vague and inexact science; there is nothing to measure or to detect it. If you spend your life in constant busyness and noise you often don't pay attention to your thoughts and visions, you could be missing a great deal of information and guidance. Such as your guides and angels giving you ideas and communications with all of nature. Depending on the mindset of each person, this filters psychic messages though that person's language, energy, beliefs and expectations. This is why one clairvoyant person can get one piece of information and another can get an entirely different bit of the jigsaw message.

Being psychic is not what I guessed it would be. I thought you would physically see things with my eyes and hear things with my ears, which apparently only a small number of psychics can do. However, for most people it is much subtler than that. You are given little mind pictures, via your imagination or words in sentences or even whole ideas, or feelings. You have to get over the fact that not all the thoughts in your mind originate from you; we are all really like transmitters and receivers. Sometimes we send out information and sometimes we receive it from outside of us. There aren't as yet many people you can go to for advice on these important things, no school where you can learn this stuff although in the future there will be many spiritual teachers and healers. It can be pretty hit and miss at the start but after a while you tend to be more aware of what is going on inside your head and start to learn which are your thoughts and what you have been receiving from outside sources. That being said, I believe we have plenty of help at hand and are guided in our learning process by our angels, spirit guides, higher-self and of course the loving Universe itself.

It is however very easy to verify to yourself whether psychic information you are getting from plants is correct. Very early on I found that I received information that could be physically checked up on and verified on the internet or in a book. I remember one time I addressed an apple tree in our garden, I said, 'How are you?' and the tree said 'come closer to me I have a surprise for you'. Intrigued, I walked up and looked around it and under a little branch I found a stem full of hidden granny smith apples. I thought all the apples were eaten by the birds but this bunch was hidden in the abundant foliage. So there was another thing that I could physically verify, the information I was receiving is not simply my imagination, making things up. They are often telling me something I don't already know. Many things can be verified one way or the other.

The idea that humans can talk to plants is quite a huge concept, there is no end to what we can find out from them. From when their fruit is going to be ripe, to what seed will turn out to be the best variety to produce the sweetest, tastiest fruit.

What is even more remarkable is I can ask them what disease or mineral deficiency they have and they give me an accurate description and what I can do for them. One day I went up to my fruit orchard looking at the trees and one poor 'Cox's Orange Pippin' apple tree looked very sad with mottled crinkled leaves for quite a few years. I asked him what was wrong with him and he gave me an image of the words boron deficiency, and a vision of a box of borax. I rushed back inside and consulted my plant diseases book and yes, a boron deficiency has exactly the symptoms that the tree had been exhibiting for a number of years. A packet of borax sprinkled onto the soil would remedy the situation, which I promptly did. I actually cured the tree of a mineral deficiency by communicating with the tree itself! A bit of insider information can come in pretty handy sometimes!

Chapter 2
The First Conversations

To discover, is to see things with new eyes.

I am addressing the gum trees outside the window of my room.

So I can talk to you even though I am not outside?

"Yes, we certainly can talk at any distance from each other as you can with other people too, you do not need to be in the same room, country or even dimension to address different things, people, souls, whatever you want to call them."

So on a broader scale how can conversing with plants help humanity?

"In many ways but mainly energetically, we are the great healers of the world, we can heal and relieve you of your negative emotions and help you feel happier within yourselves. We also hold great knowledge of medicinal healing plants, foods for good health and we house the fairy realm, who we work in tandem with in keeping the earth clean, tidy, and working as one organism."

So you know about fairies? Tell me about them.

"They are all around us, they are where plants are and some are also where plants are not. They heal and beautify and sow seeds, they are the energy behind your beloved flowers, they pollinate, cultivate and talk to the stones. They hold great knowledge of magic, plants and earth magic and manifestation. They are happy joyful creatures, if it weren't for them, we plants would not exist, and without plants you would not be able to exist. You see it is all a symbiotic relationship, one entity helps the other who helps the other."

Can you see them?

"No we don't have eyes as such but we can feel them and imagine their look and energy, we are very aware of them as we are of you."

Are they kind? Do they like humans?

"Of course they love humans very much and, in some ways, aspire to be like humans. They are the link, if you like, between the plant world and the human world, they are from both realms. They love you all very much but they wish more of you would believe in their existence, so that you could see them. Even you cannot yet see them although you know that they are there, as you fear your higher psychic talents."

Oh, so it is like in children's stories, if you don't believe in fairies as adults do, you cannot see them?

"Yes exactly, where do you think the writer got their ideas from, it was from the fairy realm? Children are more likely to see the fairies as they are more believing and delighted in what their eyes see. It is only when adults then judge what the children are seeing that the children shut down their psychic senses that enabled them to see the fairies in the first place. "

So believing and not fearing are pivotal in being able to see the fairy realm. What advantages are there for humanity to see and connect with the fairies?

"Yes, many and varied, firstly it is ignorant to not want to see what is really there. The fairies are all around you all the time anyway, you might as well know what they are doing; it is for your benefit after all. They are nature's magicians and can help your ailing river systems, lakes, seas, mountain, volcanoes, typhoons and hurricanes, bushfires, floods, food and crop health and nutrition, they can make barren land fertile, they can create miracles in nature. But they are hampered at the moment because hardly any humans are aware of them and their efforts and they need to now work in tandem with humanity if we are to bring earth's system back into balance. We cannot be separate anymore, humanity cannot keep on existing alone and get ahead without communicating with the fairies and sea nymphs, trees, plants, rocks and mountains and the wind sylphs, the rain germanders and the fire salamanders. All of these things are conscious and can be communicated with. The fairies and the whole of nature cannot progress without you humans being fully conscious and you will not be able to exist anymore on this earth without our cooperation, open communication and help."

"The fairies know how to fix all of your environmental concerns; you just need to consult with us and work with us. We (both the nature realms and humanity) need now at this point in time to work in tandem, not in isolation. Both humanity

and the fairy realms need to work towards raising their frequencies, nothing else will world to get to the new earth that is waiting for us all."

How do we raise our vibrations and how many people on earth can talk to the fairies and the trees like I can?

"How do we know? There must be millions who could immediately talk to the plants and fairies if they address them politely. Everyone is capable of it; it is just not everyone vibrates with enough love for the link to be successful."

Is it the level and quality of the love that we have in general or the love that we have for plants and fairies that enables clear communication?

"Yes of course. Love is the conduit to clear communication. Love is the conduit to everything. With love you are capable of nearly anything."

So the best thing humans can do to heal the earth is to start loving everything and everyone more, including themselves and to start talking to the plants and fairies and to start believing in fairies?

"You've got it in one."

To start to believe and start to talk to your local plants today and see what they have to say to you?

"Exactly, but don't forget the love part; this allays any fears that can hamper any communications between realms."

I guess the lesson for all of us is to suspend our disbelief and to really tune into our psychic senses?

"Yes, and to open all avenues of love, love between your fellow humans, animals, rocks, plants, situations, your life, the earth. Love clears all channels, love is everything."

I'm addressing again the gum trees just outside my window. Do other plants varieties have different personalities and do, say gum trees within the same species have different personalities?

"They are all separate entities as such and have different ages and experiences of the world. We who live near to human habitation see ourselves as very blessed to experience close human interactions and hopefully they spend some time with or near us. We learn a great deal from this and it increase our enjoyment of life, but we would still enjoy it anyway. Each plant is different."

What has most surprised me about my communications with plants is just how loving and wise they are both towards us and in life in general. I sort of thought that communicating with them would be like talking to a child-like pet however instead they are very astute, compassionate and knowledgeable.

I have been determined to have a beautiful garden all year, full of flowers, despite water prices. What do the gum trees think about the human habit of buying water and paying water bills?

"We get our water as we need it from nature itself, all else is beyond our comprehension as Mother Earth provides us with all our needs, as she does yours. When you look at it this way there is no want or restrictions, only a need supplied, because we expect to be watered and we are and when we aren't that is alright also, it is part of the plan of things. We accept whatever comes with gratitude. You humans should really take a few leaves out of our book".

Addressing the gum trees again. So you practice gratitude as part of getting what you need?

"Yes, but also getting into the flow of nature and the Universe it is more joyful being in the flow rather than resisting it, which is what causes you humans so much unnecessary pain and discomfort, being grateful for whatever comes even if it is not exactly what you planned or expected, as everything is all alright in the grand scheme of things."

Do plants feel emotions like humans?

"Yes, but we often choose our higher thoughts and therefore attract and produce the higher emotional response to situations. We would be of no use to you humans if we went around like you did, producing negative responses and emotion willy-nilly sullying the atmosphere wherever you go. This is not all humans of course, but most. Part of our role is to help cleanse the earth of emotions that are not in everyone's best interest. We cleanse the air, the atmosphere, other plants and the water-ways and animals and people themselves. Just by going outside you naturally are refreshed and cleansed by whatever plants are in your vicinity."

So people that live in built-up big cities would be at a disadvantage because of the lack of plants around them?

"They are at a major disadvantage in many respects, the least of which are not having trees and plants to clear the air and water and food of pollution and thought pollution. This is why city people are often sicker, angrier and more violent towards each other and have shortened lifespans because of pollution. Cities are not ideal places to live in as even the good ones that are clean and have trees in them, do not have enough balance of vegetation to buildings to make them sustainable. The

plant life needs to be dense and natural in order to house the maximum of fairies or nature angels to keep the areas clean and clear."

Do plants feel the heat and cold like humans?

"Yes of course we also feel a broader range of things like humans are capable of doing, but do not do so at the moment. We know of the presence of spiritual visitations from other dimensions, we can see and sense auras and thoughts from plants and animals and people. We can sense what the climate is going to do so we also don't worry in that way that you humans do about the weather forecast, because we have enough advance warning about say a flood so we can prepare ourselves for lots of rain by starting our new growth systems or by closing down some of our root absorption systems. We also close down our systems when we have advance notice of extreme heat-waves or cold spans and also excessive windstorms".

Fragrance

Working in the garden for me is like painting one giant picture with flowers, foliage and form except this picture is a three dimensional one that I can walk into, touch, smell and interact with. Like a living, breathing work of art.

I asked the Euryops daisies what is the purpose of flowers?

"Well there is the bee and pollinator attractant role and then there is the beauty for beauty sake role. We make flowers to display our love to the world. This is why the colours and forms are so exuberant, they are for display, for fun and for joy, not purely utilitarian but a little bit of both".

Passionfruit-scented marigold plants, what is the role of flower fragrance?

"Flower fragrance is both to get the flowers pollinated and to communicate with plants, insects and humans. We communicate happiness, joy, peace and love via our perfumes".

Fragrance is love, in a scent.

Do different fragrances mean different things?

"Different fragrances attract different pollinators but also communicate different forms of love to all who behold the scent. Scent is not really a thing to know, but to feel and experience. Once you smell a beautiful fragrance you need not know anything else about it, just feel it. Let the fragrance work its magic on you".

Is fragrance holy?

"There is nothing on this earth that is not holy but yes fragrance is holy in that respect and is priceless in its value to all who experience it. It is capable of lifting moods, heightening awareness and giving inspiration and inspiring love. Is that not holy?"

Yes, it is. Are plants aware of the sun and moon? Do you gain other advantages from leaning towards the moon?

"The moon is essential for life as we know it on earth. We get the suns reflected energy from the moon and move along with the moons cycles too. The sun and moon are responsible for of all the natural cycles on this planet."

Are you aware when we put fertilizer on you and water and prune and tend you?

"Of course we do as soon as the fertilizer reaches our roots, we are able to use it but we are aware as you put it on. We are even aware of when you think about fertilizing us and reach for the manure packet in the shed. We can anticipate your moves for our welfare. We enjoy very much the act of being watered; it clears our cells and refreshes our leaves, allowing us to breathe more clearly. We accept pruning and are revived after a while when we can be relieved of our load of too much old growth or dead wood. We like it when you assist our functioning in such ways".

Eucalyptus trees 'What does it do to the land and ecosystems and us humans to have a once forested land left with only a few remaining trees'?

"It saddens the land and all who inhabit it even if they do not realize it. It gives them a sadness of countenance and a yearning for a land that is whole and nourished and replenished with enough tree and shrub growth to maintain its ecosystems. We need not go into all the environmental and air quality problems, that you are well aware of."

Confirmation

I'm starting to appreciate being able to communicate with plants. It has its definite benefits for a gardener. There are often times when a plant is ailing and you don't know what is wrong or what to do about it. Or a plant is attacked by some animal but you don't know what. It is definitely handy to know how many fruits are on a tree or when they'll be ripe by simply asking the tree. I am no longer working in the dark as to what is going on in my garden and it has come in very handy! Just yesterday I questioned a carnation plant as to what was eating it and had a vision of rabbits. So then I knew at night they were getting a thorough chewing from our little furry friends. The lawn in the front garden was getting a chewing in summer, I asked the grass and it responded back giving me a mind picture of rabbits and chickens too eating my grass. Sure enough one morning a few days later I saw a small rabbit out of the corner of my eye on the grass. Over and over again I get confirmation that what the plants have told me is indeed correct, it is not simply my imagination.

A Raining and a Humming

It's hailing today. Delicious dark brooding skies loom overhead, yielding intermittent hail showers, then suddenly the sun makes an appearance. Very nice, I enjoy the rain, even in iced form!

Trees, I was wondering do plants like hail?

"Yes, hail and rain are the same forces; we find them very refreshing they clear our leaves and stomata's so that we can take in the sun's rays more clearly. Hail is invigorating."

What do you do or think of when it rains?

"We celebrate of course. We hum and sing, it is a joyful thing for us to experience especially if it has been a while between showers. We soak it up through our roots and it washes all the cells in our leaves. We are left feeling refreshed and renewed.

The miracle of rain is life itself.

Do you have conversations with other plants?

"Yes of course but mainly we sing, hum and vibrate, create vibrations of love and joy. Other plants do the same and we know which plants are doing it according to their different vibrations."

Can you hear us sing and talk?

"Not really but we feel your vibrations and moods and know your thoughts telepathically. We understand most of what is said if it is clearly said in the mind, we don't pick up sound as such."

What is it when we humans go outside that is good for us? I asked the trees one morning.

"The solution is threefold one it is the goodness of breathing in fresh and not stale air, this brings in fresh solutions to problems where you could only come up with stale ones sitting inside. The inspiration of air emits true inspiration literally and figuratively. Two is the healing effect of the sun, it clears the air of any negative thoughts you have picked up."

"There is the profound healing effect of the plants and fairies on the human aura. The fairies' role is to keep the plant systems and human systems working harmoniously. If anything is out of balance, they make it their duty to clear it. Plus, the healing effect of nature on your senses, eyes seeing all the colours and green of the foliage. Nature's healing sounds, touch and feelings calms the human body and mind."

How do plants have such wisdom that humanity seems to have lost or not be in touch with?

"We have not removed ourselves from our roots and our own instinctive guidance. We trust our instincts, guidance and higher information and operate on it at all times. Most humans ignore their guidance as secondary information instead of primary information like it is supposed to be."

What do plants think of human inventions such as tractors and houses?

"We love all human inventions; they are part of human existence and as such are a positive thing. Even if at times they can be destructive. Destruction is also part of nature's systems and life cycles."

Do plants have a sense of time or are they living in the present moment?

"We only live in the present moment, there is no need to do anything else."

Do plants have emotions like humans?

"*Not exactly the same but we feel things and have compassion and love and friendship. We care for the world around us but we don't go around hating others like humans do, which is not our role. We like to add positivity to the atmosphere to cleanse it to make the world to a better place, not a worse one.*"

Are plants intelligent like humans and animals?

"*Not as intelligent as humans but more intelligent sometimes when it comes to matters of the spirit and using one's insight and gut feelings, plants are better adapted to do this. All plants are equal, there is none more intelligent than another but there are plants that hold more experience because of their advanced age and experience.*"

Native Versus Non-Native

It is one of those fabulous still sunny afternoons again. I couldn't help but spend most of the afternoon outside. I planted more wattle bushes for a windbreak. Gum trees, what do you think about having native verses non-native plants in the garden?

"Naturally we prefer you to plant natives to whatever region you live in but we understand that decorative gardens give much peace and pleasure to humans and as such welcome all plants into the garden equally. It is the quality of the love that is important. If you really love those plants then it is good to plant them, if you love others, plant them. Do you see?'

Yes, I do, we should do and plant what brings us the most joy.

"Yes indeed."

There is no greater place than in a garden, where the fairies fly and dreams soar. On a fine day, everything seems possible.

Chapter 3
Our Outside Eyes and Ears

You are never alone in nature, there is always something that sees you and loves you for being you.

It suddenly occurred to me what other advantages there are to being able to talk to the greenery. You could certainly get the inside-knowledge on other things that are going on around the place. They are our outside eyes and ears. You could ask them what has been going on in your garden in your absence. This occurred to me as I passed a vandalized street tree while out driving this morning. The tree itself could explain what happened to it and who did it. The world is alive and conscious, there is nothing that doesn't get witnessed on some level or another, there really are no secrets.

The implications of this are huge. The fact that all greenery, all plants are intelligent and conscious and can be communicated with about anything is very important. Trees and plants are certainly aware of what's going on around them and because they are also comfortably super-conscious, they know about things that are not in their immediate experience and circumstance.

I wonder if you could find missing things by asking a tree, say where a missing pair of pruners are? I'll have to try that some time.

I asked the trees: What did you think about the drier seasons we have been getting lately and now this really beautiful wet one?

"We don't think in terms of wet and dry, we take what we get when we get it, we enjoy it all and respond accordingly, if we get less rain we draw in less moisture and put on less growth and stop the growth earlier in the year. We adapt, like a

boat flowing along with the flow of the stream, we don't go against the stream by resisting what is. What is 'is', and as such it is beautiful, the whole of life is beautiful and we make the most of what we get when we get it. We don't waste time on thinking on what might have been. All that we get is what we want. Why would we desire what we didn't get, that is wasted energy?"

Fabulous, love it! I asked the gum trees: Do you communicate at all with the fairies or the land itself?

"Yes, we communicate all the time with the fairies and also to the spirits of the land."

What do you talk about?

"We talk about how we are growing and when the different insects and birds are coming in and about our roots and branches and leaves and other tree issues. We also talk about the weather and about the fairies' issues and lives.'

Do plants ever gossip?

"If talking about one's personal issues then yes, if you mean talking meanly and judgmentally about others, then no."

The Joy of Flowers

The front garden with its proliferation of daisies and well, daisies, and has burst into clouds of cheerfulness! My husband mowed the lawn yesterday and the flat green carpet sets off the mass daisy flowers superbly. It even has the fragrance of spring, like something deliciously sweet on the gently warmed breeze.

I asked the trees why it would be that I am so attracted to flowers in particular?

"Flowers carry the love of God and all things in God's Universe, pure, essential, satisfying love on all levels. Unconditional love and profuse joy for all things, is what flowers display for us, so it is no wonder that the more sensitive among us are very much drawn to their beauty and grace."

Do different flowers display different concepts of love and joy?

"Love is love and joy is joy no matter how it is displayed all flowers represent such things but have their specialties in what other emotional states they like to inspire such as contentment, peace, wonder and humour."

What do the flowers of your tree represent or inspire in us?

"Beauty of the world of bees and wasps and what good service they render to the whole of the world in pollinating all our plants producing more fruit vegetables seeds, nuts and baby plants. Without their generous and loyal service all these things that humans take for granted would not happen. You humans need to show more gratitude for the insects of the world by not spraying chemicals indiscriminately and ultimately coming up with better ways to eliminate pests and disease damage on crops and gardens. A garden is a place that displays a love and reverence for all of life, not just little pockets if it here and there but the broad spectrum of all there is, as each small part contributes to the wellbeing of the whole. Eliminate one part and you are in danger of destroying parts of the rest too. Man needs to learn that all parts of nature are essential for balance and the law of balance means that this is what man needs to introduce into their garden and crop technologies."

Does it improve the atmosphere of the garden the more flowers there are in a garden?

"Yes of course we all have flowers for the contribution they make to the overall peace and happiness and harmony of an area. The more flowers there are the more peaceful, happy and harmonious the garden is. Who could stay grumpy or sad in a garden full of flowers? If the flowers are brought indoors in huge bunches, then the atmosphere inside the home is improved greatly with more harmonious relations between people, and peaceful and happy feelings encouraged."

Flower Fragrance

It fills me with joy to enter my garden and to smell the welcoming distinctive fragrance that smells like, my garden! My favourite flowers combine is a delicious signature scent that I always remember come springtime. I grow things just as much for their fragrance as I do for their colour. I asked the freesias: What are the roles of flower scents to humans in the garden?

"Fragrances lift the vibrational frequencies of an area, garden or room. If the fragrance is of a natural origin, preferably floral, then there are certain blessings attached to smelling it. It heightens the thoughts of humans in the vicinity and helps soothe bad moods or argumentative residents. Fragrance is also a bridge

between the human and angelic worlds and helps communication between species. Do not underestimate the power of fragrance; it can change the mood and situation in whole regions. All while the residents remain oblivious to the fragrance's pivotal importance in the natural world. Without fragrance the world would be a poorer place."

"Fragrance helps lighten one's mood and countenance and helps lift depression and lethargy. Fragrance plays a big role in why people are more energetic in spring once all the flowers in blossom come out en-masse."

Flower Colour

What are the roles of flower and leaf colour in the garden and to humans?

"Yes, colour is a powerful mood enhancer that your human civilization is about to realize. Colours and different tones of the same colour have different effects on the human psyche and emotions. Colours can calm you down, excite you, heal you, please you, challenge you and add to higher qualities such as peace, love, joy happiness and fulfilment in your lives. Colour enhances the effect of fragrance on a person depending on the qualities that that plant specializes in."

I asked the rose bushes: Do you like the birds?

"We love the birds, they are our great friends and companions and facilitators. They help us pollinate, create movement and blessings for us. We enjoy immensely being of service when a bird chooses to have a nest in us. We consider it an honour to shelter birds and animals."

Chapter 4

Taking in the Qualities of a Region by Eating It's Produce

You can tell the qualities of a man by the qualities of the food he eats.

Broccoli plants I read somewhere that it is better for people to eat what is grown in their area from their particular climate and soils for maximum health benefits. Do you know anything about this?

"Yes, we know that humans eating locally say within ten or twenty or a hundred kilometres away, produced from within that area has put up with the same climatic effects that you are likely to experience too and has grown strong in such a climate. Eating this gives those properties such as making you strong in that particular climate. Do you see?"

Yes, I think so, thank you.

The broccoli went on:

"Like eating something that gives you a built-in resistance to the negative effects of such a climate such as lots of wind or very hot temperatures. You then inherit this built-in resistance by consuming a food plant that experiences the climate which you live with in your region."

So if for instance someone ate only things grown in a tropical region but lived in the cool mountains. They wouldn't be eating and taking in the qualities that give them some resistance to their cold climate, they would only be preparing themselves for a tropical one. A very interesting topic. This is yet another and perhaps the most compelling reason yet to grow local and eat local produce.

Gum trees, do trees use time as measurement at all?

"Only when talking to people."

Do you hear our music when I sing?

"We don't hear it as such but we feel its vibrations and enjoy it. We love it when humans sing. It means they on some level are happy and express themselves in a meaningful way."

Rose Pruning

Roses, do you mind being pruned in winter?

"No we don't mind as was said before, we feel freed from restrictive old growth. We welcome the feeling or renewal that a prune gives us."

Does it hurt?

"We feel it but we have ways of protecting ourselves from pain and put our sap to other areas of our plant. As soon as it's done, we proceed with the healing process."

I can feel spring in the air; an excited anticipation that things are building up, ready to bloom and grow. I asked a rose bush whether they find they put on better flower displays one year compared to another?

"All years are good years for us, we cannot compare our flower displays as we only really live in the moment, the display we have is the best so far as we are concerned. Whatever is happening now is always the best for us. We neither look forward nor backwards like you humans seem to do. Every flower display is Divine and beautiful, how can we compare it, it is like comparing children?"

Do plants enjoy spring more than any other season?

"There is a certain joy when all the plants are flowering at the same time, it is like a mass celebration, but we do not have any favourite season they are all Divine for us. Spring is fun however for its unique qualities."

Can you hear the roosters crowing?

"We sense their vibrations and harmony."

Do you feel the bees going from flower to flower?

"Yes, we certainly do, it tickles and we especially enjoy it, we make our flowers specially to attract the bees and other pollinating insects."

Are plants psychic?

"Yes of course we are, how else do you think we can talk to you and other plants and insects?"

What is Happening to the Bees of the World?

Gum trees what is causing the loss of the bee populations especially in the northern hemisphere?

"The changing of chemicals to harsher broad-acre varieties that wipe out weed seeds, the pre-emergent ones are affecting the pupae life cycle of the bees, wasps, beetles, frogs, flycatchers, in fact all insect larvae within five kilometres of spraying. If they want food crops in the future, they must stop using these chemicals."

Thank you. I have been wondering what was going on there. So what can the average person do about this problem?

"Stop using chemicals personally and only purchase organic produce from supermarkets, shops and markets, insist on it. Refuse to have any part in the willful wholesale destruction of the delicate insect/plant balance of the planet. Be or 'bee' part of the solution and not the problem!"

That was funny, that could be used or 'bee' used as a slogan to help save or planet's food supply amongst other things. I didn't know plants could joke!

Are there any things we can do or plant in our garden to encourage more bees?

"Yes do not use any chemicals in the garden bees are very vulnerable to them and plant as many bee attracting plants as possible from annuals to perennials, trees and shrubs. There are hosts of varieties that will attract, feed and support small local bee populations saving them from distinction. Do not be scared if bees decide to build a hive near you, be honoured, they will not sting you if you beam them love. They know who you are and will only bring good luck to your garden and property.'

"'If there are beehives there then the fairies have deemed it fit that they needed a local hive there to better service the plants. Embrace nature in all its forms."

The evening after writing this I was sitting outside and reading a book under a tree and a lovely native bee flew over and hovered above the book page, almost stationary in the air above the page as though he was talking to me, thanking me even, for my chapter on bees. I beamed love at him and he flew off.

Where there are bees, there is life.

Chapter 5
Thankfulness and the Energy of Transaction

To be thankful is to say yes to life.

Broccoli plants is it beneficial to thank the plants as we harvest things from them for our own use? Does this change the nature of the vegetable harvested?

"Yes, indeed plants, animals and humans and all parts of nature respond positively to gratitude. The energy of thankfulness changes the nature of the plants or animal being harvested and eaten, making it more healthful for humans to eat and more beneficial for the plants to heal itself and move on or whatever the case maybe. This means there has been an equal exchange of energy; you have taken a piece of broccoli and have given thankfulness in return. You can thank plants or animals in your mind by appreciating the produce or saying it out loud. A 'thank you' said out loud is always beneficial. It is the law of exchange, of giving and receiving which is in effect here."

Broccolis, are there certain qualities with food plants which, when you eat them, you take on those qualities?

"No your character remains the same, but if you are that way inclined you will feel more peaceful when eating lettuce and more thoughtful when eating an apple. These are enhancements to what is already there not traits that can be gleaned from scratch."

What happens if you don't thank the flowers and plants for the food and produce?

"Nothing, but the beneficial effects on the body, and nutrition are significantly lessened and the beneficial effects of the flowers brought inside is lessened, but not stopped altogether. One almost automatically appreciates a bunch of flowers when

it is picked for instance so in this way it almost never happens, but with commercial crops there is a serious issue of taking from the plants and the land and nature without giving back respect and thankfulness. The scale that crops are put in and taken away, without due care and love is affecting human nutrients and land fertility en-masse."

So you are saying that we as farmers, gardeners and say market-gardeners need to thank and be grateful as we harvest the crops, is this where harvest festivals came from?

"Yes, exactly that is where the whole idea of harvest thankfulness dinners and celebrations came from. In countries and areas where this is still a feature, they still have kept their fertile soils."

How thankful do you need to be say for a large crop being harvested?

"Very thankful, so if every person who harvests it gave thanks and appreciation, that is enough."

What about the buyer of say produce from a market? Do they need to be thankful for their purchase of fresh produce? What about value-added produce such as bread and cakes that are made from natural products?

"Yes, and yes if one is thankful for what one has just purchased whether it be from the natural world or not, the energy transaction is not completed properly. If an item is bought and no thanks is given and then complaints are made then negativity is brought into the transaction making either the product not work so well or making you dissatisfied every time you use it, not benefiting the consumer at all."

So thankfulness need not be saying 'thank you' out loud, it could simply be loving or liking the product you just bought?

"Exactly, but the more grateful and happy you are with the purchase or transaction of energy the greater the benefits you will get from that product throughout the lifetime of its use. So if you were say grateful for a shirt the moment you bought it. It would give a certain level of benefits but if you are grateful and happy with it every time you wear it will give you blessings every time you wear it. As you know, this is a lot of what the Chinese technique of feng shui was based upon."

What if someone is neutral about a product?

"Then they would get neutral benefits. If one's dislikes or hates a product say a car, then the car will only give them problems. That is why it is important to be *grateful and thankful for everything in your life be it alive or inanimate because everything is made up of conscious energy and responds to your thoughts."*

Yes, indeed cars, washing machines, computers, and even houses could all benefit from this psychic gratefulness service!

Plant Gratitude

Do plants practice gratitude on a daily basis?

"We do not need to practice it is as such as it is our natural state, we are grateful for every moment of every day and for whatever we get. That is our role; ours is not to judge and question and hypothesize like you humans. We simply be, in love and in joy."

To be in joy is to be lovingly present.

Aren't there ever times when you are unhappy?

"That would presume that we don't live in the present moment where we can compare this moment with the last one, we had, or one we might have in the future. We love in the now and we accept what is here at this moment and deal and adapt to each thing as it comes up. We do feel distress when we are ill or the environment is out of whack or another plant, animal or human is in distress. However, once we have dealt with it, it is over, we do not dwell in an unhappy state, looking at what might have been. We accept and move on. Our role is healers of the planet, that would not happen if we were creating psychic and energetic garbage too, it would be counter-productive."

Telepathy

I asked the gum trees: Can all people communicate with plants in the same way that I can?

"Yes of course, it is just that you are more sensitive and aware of the message and thoughts you are getting and where they are coming from. All people can go out today and ask a tree a question either in their mind or out loud and will be met with a response. People must understand that the response is not simply their imagination. Your imagination is the movie screen that links you to All There Is. You can both put your own wants and desires into it and let the Universe know

that is what you want by accompanying it with joyful feelings. Your imagination is also the screen wherein you get messages telepathically from your own guidance and other people and other things like messages from plants, animals, rocks, whatever it is you would like to talk to, can communicate back via mental images which is called telepathy."

Does each different plant and stone for instance have a different personality?

"Of course we are as different from each other as you are from another person, similar but with different likes and dislikes and experiences.'"

So any person can today walk right up to a plant and can receive some sort of communication from it?

"Yes of course, one must of course be aware of the thoughts that cross their minds and one must kindly address the plant, but apart from that there is no reason why everyone can't start communicating between species."

Will what everyone gets telepathically be accurate?

"Well it is as accurate as the vessel, messages can only come through your mind with all of its prejudices and beliefs, so what one person gets from one tree may be different from what another person gets. In the same way that one person may ask another person a question and get one answer and come to certain conclusions about it and a second person may ask the same person a question and seem to get a different response and draw different conclusions from the same or similar answer."

"Telepathy works by using your own known store of images, known facts, words and known ideas. If say a person had never seen a bucket for example, then it would be hard for a tree to talk to them about a bucket if they hadn't even had a mental picture of one. We can only be artists with the palette of what you already know and are aware of. Otherwise the images would be meaningless."

"This is why a book like this is important because it opens the door of possibility, letting people know what is possible. If they never knew they could talk to plants and animals in their minds they would never attempt it. Belief is also the bridge between this world of solid reality and all other possible realities. Many more things are possible for humans if they only believe it was possible. This is what is going to happen in a few years the gates of belief are going to be thrown wide open and your own lives and possibilities are going to be extended beyond what you currently think is possible. It is going to be a wondrous and beautiful time for you all."

SARAH RAJKOTWALA

Thank you, that was beautiful and very enlightening.

Chapter 6
Flowers

Flowers are the happy face of nature.

It is another glorious day; all the daisy bushes look so joyful on an overcast day. The fragrances of spring fills the air with such beauty that my heart sings with joy.

Daisies, does the mass planting of one plant variety increase the effect on an environment and the people in the garden?

"Yes, indeed it multiplies by ten the effects of say one plant. The main effects are exacerbated to good effect and are a very positive thing to do in a garden. So if one plant variety encourages peaceful feelings, many plants of the same bush would give an inherent feeling of peacefulness in that area and garden. This is the way plant communities operate and their reason for their being where they are. It is the groups and combined groups of plantings that are of great benefit to the humans and animal residents of the area."

Roses how does it affect a person when they go into a garden full of the same sort of flowers, say a rose?

"A person is filled with the sorts of thoughts and feelings that those flowers fragrance and colours exemplify. With roses for instance a person soaks up the frequencies of love quite strongly. You can never come out of a flower and rose garden grumpy or out-of-sorts, you will always feel more uplifted, more loving, happy and hopeful. Roses represent and beam out the frequency of love, love of God, love of self, love of others and your environment. Roses are the floral representation of love."

Roses do different varieties teach different aspects of love with their different forms, colours and scents?

"This would be true. Red roses represent the passion side of love. Pink, the nurturing side of love. White the pure innocent side of love, yellow the fun-loving side, orange the free-thinking side, violet the spiritual side. Plus, many other combinations and permutations within the colour ranges."

"The different scents also teach and encourage different aspects of love too. You'd need to speak to each individual rose about its own form of scent and what it represents."

What about the mass use of certain flower and leaf colours, does the increased amount have increased desirable effects?

"Yes, it does and so does the fragrance, one bush is beneficial and more than that bathes the area in goodness and wellbeing. This is why people feel so good in gardens, and park and forests, so calm, inspiring and peaceful at the same time. This is also why areas with few plants don't feel that good and are stressful and unkind to the senses."

"You could play with making gardens that are designed for particular feelings to be experienced like a love garden or a peace garden or an inspiration garden. You are talented at garden design and could design such places with quite a lot of beauty."

Yes, I could, I have been thinking about doing such a thing, thanks.

Roses, does the qualities of one rose variety differ from another rose variety?

"Yes, it does, some have more scent, with different tones which affects different senses in a different way. A red rose would lend you the feelings of love, boldness and excitement whereas a pure white one would inspire feelings of calmness, peace and serenity. The bulk planting of one variety would increase the rose's effects on a garden atmosphere."

Roses do you plants like pets in the garden?

"Not like love, we love the movement and fun that the pets can bring and also the sense of them needing us for shelter and climbing on. We love being of use to people and animals."

So do you like being of use to humans too?

"In any way we can provide shelter, food flowers, fodder, building materials etc. We think there is no higher honour than to serve humanity in this way. It is

why we are here and helps us to become a part of something larger. We love to be of use and service."

Do the fairies love to be of service too?

"Yes of course, we are all part of the greater whole and are really all spun out of the same yarn, so to speak. What helps one person helps us all. We plants and the fairies are quite sensitive and can feel the beneficial effects that helping a human or animal can bring. They also consider it an honour and a fun thing to be of service to humans as well as nature, so they often do what they can for any human who goes out in nature."

Who Is it I Am Talking to When I Talk to the Plants?

Gum trees what are the benefits of gardening to human beings?

"There is the value of fresh air exercise, the ions from the water and wind and the beneficial effects of working closely with the plants, fairies and other nature angels that all exist to make the environment better for humans to enjoy life on earth. There is also the value of the scents, sight and sounds of nature and stretching bending and regularly keeping your body in good form. There is also the prosperity factor where you are always prosperous when you have a garden full of plants and animals and birds to gladden the senses. A place for solace and reflection, for study and learning. There is the beneficial value of the sun, moon, sunrises and sunsets that humans are only just finding out about. When one can grow one's own food and flowers one has prosperity of a kind that simply can't be bought, it is a prosperity of the soul, of the generosity of nature and all its gifts. Humans have much to learn from nature and the trees, the mountains. The outdoors is a natural and health-giving school room, a perfect place to socialize and have fun. All social activities, games, and lessons are heightened when they are conducted out-of-doors. There is a spiritual element that heightens the experience and takes it out of the ordinary.'

'There is the value of people getting together for nature and in nature such as community gardening, shared gardens, home gardens, social gardens, parks and

nature strips, it is all important to the human's psyche and soul. Without nature there would be no humans and animals."

I asked the gum trees: How do you cope with air pollution?

"We are nature's pollution cleaners and air filters so it is one of our jobs to produce clear fresh air, we do this s number of ways but the end result is clean air for all to breathe and enjoy."

"The shrubs are like natures lint filters and slow down and stop erosion and airborne dust and particles and capture it and collect it on the ground to be turned into topsoil." '

"Groundcovers are nature's face masks keeping the soil below moist and fertile."

"Climbers are nature's air-conditioners keeping the air moist and vital as it passes through their growth. "

"Grasses are nature's pollinators and ground cooling devices, keeping the topsoil at a regular temperature so that all who reside in it can survive and thrive like insects, frogs, lizards, worms and other plants."

I asked the gum trees when I am talking to you and other plants, am I addressing you, the plant soul or a plant fairy?

"Yes, all three. You are addressing the plant spirit or fairy called a fawn or sprite. As such we have fairy powers of divination and manifestation. This is why we get along so well with the fairies because of this link. We are all part of nature as are human beings after all."

Dear gum trees, when I am talking to the plants, am I sometimes getting answers from fairies?

"Yes and no. Yes, the souls of plants are part of the fairy realms, but no you are only being answered by a fairy if you address one in the first place."

Gum trees if they were aware of my husband walking and painting the garden furniture?

"Yes of course we are, we sense him. We know what he is doing by the tone of his thoughts. We can see his thought pictures and sometimes his words. He is enjoying what he is doing at the moment (except for the wind) even though he didn't relish the prospect at the start."

Did you know I was down in the rose garden weeding?

"We are aware of everything around us, the birds, bees, trucks and motorbikes, the planes overhead and people passing, the animals, the wind, the rain, the hail. We are aware of it all and can communicate with it all, if the subjects want to."

Do you feel heat and cold like we humans do?

"Yes, but instead of putting on more coverings we alter our cells and stomata's and leaf hairs to trap warm air around our leaves or close down our systems a little whichever is most appropriate."

Do you prepare yourselves ahead of time or as the heat or cold sets in?

"Sometimes ahead of time, if it is a big cold front coming in and other times at the time."

Do you know our every human change of mood, idea and feeling?

"Yes, you can do the same with each other, you just don't know you can. In fact, you often pick up on and mirror them and think they are your own. You can also pick up on our thoughts, the thoughts of the fairies, animals, birds, the breeze, the hill etc. There aren't strict rigid boundaries in life like it appears, there is always a sharing and exchange between forms and spirit. It's just that you can't see it."

Do the plants have favourite things that humans do?

"Interesting question, I suppose any human contact with us is always welcome and interesting. We like it when you sing, talk and love. Yes, we can feel your love emanating out of you. We love it when you interact with each other. We love any sort of attention and tending you give to either us or the surrounding garden."

"Appreciation, we can feel your appreciation, it is good for us. So that is much appreciated also. Dancing and play are also fun for us as are you bringing pets and wildlife into the garden. Parties and get-togethers, we also like them. People spending time in the garden to maintain it is also nice. Basically any sort of activity you do out in the garden is also enjoyable for the plants to sense and experience and observe too."

Are you aware of what we are doing in the house, do you notice it?

"Yes, we know when you are in there and what you are thinking and feeling. We know when you go out and where you are going and what you are thinking when you are going there too."

I asked the roses, do the fairies sow plants in the gaps of bare soil?

"Yes of course who else? They choose the right variety, scatter the seeds, water and tend them. Nothing is accidental."

So in a garden such as mine with lots of flowers and plant varieties in it would have more fairies in it, than say a garden with a few evergreen shrubs and a manicured lawn?

"Of course flowers equal fairies. Each flower owns at least one fairy, maybe more. So the more flower plants there are the more fairies in the air and on the ground tending them. They add to the general atmosphere of wellbeing. That's why garden with lots of flowers make you feel so happy and buoyant."

Are the fairies out all day and night or more at one time than another?

"More night than day, lots in the evening when the flowers need to be closed in the morning when they need to be opened up again."

Do fairies live in the garden, do they sleep there? Where do they go on say a cold and rainy day?

"They aren't entirely of this dimension so they can flit from one to the other if the need arises. They sleep and live in cozy out-of-the way areas, in the garden, parks or natural scrubland. They don't like to be exposed to the elements all the time, like humans when they choose to go indoors. Fairies sleep late at night and early in the morning, existing on less sleep than humans. They have lots of work to do and can't waste it sleeping all the night."

Are there more fairies in native gardens than any other garden type?

"Yes, fairies love natives the best, there are native fairies and ones that come with any introduced plants. There are different varieties of fairies, hundreds of thousands of different sorts as varied as the plant world and nature herself. Flower gardens have the most fairies closely flowed by wild and natural gardens that are overgrown, slightly messy with lots of hidden nooks and crannies, resting places, ponds to bathe in, birdbaths and the like. Fairies love the element of water in the garden and love every garden to have at least one birdbath or small pond."

Overcast Days and Visiting Fairies

Hooray today is one of my favourite sorts of spring days with brooding overcast skies, threatening to burst forth into rain any minute but just holding back in that delicious stillness before the storm.

Gum trees, are there some fairies that just visit your garden and others that live there permanently?

"Yes, exactly many come to your garden for the spring because here are so many flowers and plants to tend, but over half stay around and are permanent residents of your garden. Some are large nature angels more the size of a small child and

*others are a little larger, some are the size of a pencil, some walk and most fly with
some sort of wings. Some just appear and disappear as if by magic going from their
other dimension to this.*"

I asked a daisy bush: Do plants learn and mature as they grow older?

"*Of course they do, they start off young and innocent like babies but gradually
build experience and know-how. The oldest trees know a great deal of things and
are very wise beings.*"

Lichen

Addressing a weeping standard rose: Is the lichen on you bothering you at
all?

"*No not at all, it keeps the moisture in my stems and keeps good bacteria in.
It helps with warm and chilling weather to insulate the bark. We have a symbiotic
relationship; they (the lichen) use my height and my bark. I use their insulation
properties to protect my outer layer.*"

Why do we often see the most lichen around the dead branches on the fruit
trees?

"*Because they are the oldest parts, they would have died in that time-span
whether they were with lichen or without. Lichen is noticeable because of the age of
the plants and the starkness of dead branches.*"

So lichen does not harm the tree whatsoever?

"*None at all, in fact it benefits.*

SARAH RAJKOTWALA

Chapter 7

The Energy Footprint of Thankfulness in our Food Chain

Gratitude is an energetic prayer

The Footprint of Intention

Gum trees, can you tell me the difference between human food produced with love and gratitude and the food grown without love?

"There is a world of difference from the food's inception, the way the plants grow in the soil to the way it produces its crop. This in turn affects the amount and nutrition of the final crops to what effect they have in the human digestive system."

Is blessing and praying over the food we eat sufficient to make it good for us?

"Only if it was grown with respect love and gratitude in the first place. Things can't be hidden anymore; you can't cheat the energy of things and their initial intention is becoming more obvious for all to see. A business built on love and a desire to serve themselves and humanity in an honest way will always prosper and succeed. Whereas if an identical business were built on dishonesty, abuse and exploitation of its staff and a selfish greed then it will not very attractive for people to do business with and it will not succeed."

"It is not only the act itself, but the initial intentions behind it that are becoming obvious. It's like the energetic footprint of all the energy and thought put into a project or product are now open for all too see. Things can't be hidden anymore. Foods that are produced with chemicals and by not respecting the environment will not be good for people to eat whereas identical foods that are

produce with love and respect for the environment and the plants and animals will be good for people.'

So not only does it need to be a pure product but has to have pure intentions?

"If the land and the plants are thanked and treated with kindness and respect then everything will work out well."

Will they be able to digest it properly or will they have problems digesting and processing the nutrients?

"Without being grateful and blessing the crop and thanking the plants and the land the food will prove hard to digest and will cause widespread food allergies."

"Food that has been respected and the land and the plants thanked is easy to digest and is good for the human system and doesn't produce multiple food allergies in the general population."

"Humans can no longer be unconscious in the way they produce, pack and distribute food, the whole process needs to be done with respect for the land, the plants, the animals, the humans working the crops, the transporters, how they are transported and packed in natural packaging with thanks for the plants and machines that produced the packaging. You see what I mean? Each part of the process of food production is important for the end result being hopefully fresh and nutritious food that the humans can eat and fully digest their goodness."

Does it matter when digesting food whether it has been fertilized naturally or with chemicals?

"The natural way releases the most nutrients into the human systems. Chemicals produce artificial results, resulting in abnormal growth that is devoid of certain nutrients both for the plant itself and for later human consumption. Plus chemical fertilizers and pesticides pollute the land they were taken from and all its connecting ecosystems, that contributes nothing good energetically to the consumed product and could even be detrimental to human systems in the short and long term. Resulting in certain vitamin deficiencies even though sufficient food has been eaten, producing fat people that are undernourished."

Is it sufficient just to grow the food plants organically or do we have to thank the plants and land too or it won't be good?

"Organically grown food is growing it the way nature intended it, it is always good but for the cycle of food from the paddock to the plate to be complete, the thanks must now be given. Where before you could get away without it, now it is

the essential ingredient because of the finer and truer energies of this new age we are living in."

Is it enough to be quietly grateful for the crop or do we have to openly thank it?

"Either is sufficient but a formal thanks either said out loud or in your mind is the best way, and why would you not want to thank the plants when they have produced food and produce so well for you."

Yes, I agree. Now we know plants are conscious, then why wouldn't we thank them like we would any friend or worker who has done such good work for our benefit?

Are there any other things we need to thank for their good services, like the clouds for producing such good rain for us or the sun for the lovely sunny day or even inanimate objects? I have started thanking my car for driving so well for me.

"Yes, you have got the idea, everything has some level of consciousness, thank what has given you good service to secure the supply of more is always a good idea. It is like balancing out a mathematical equation, if the other side is not equal, then the act is not complete. Nature always seeks to balance itself."

If we don't thank the plants for a good crop what are the possible consequences?

"The line of energy follows through; no thanks and gratefulness at one end could reduce its efficiency and continued supply at the other. Maybe a reduced crop the next year? Maybe the food would not last as well and would go off sooner, maybe it wouldn't sell as well, maybe it wouldn't digest as well."

What about cut flowers, what would happen then?

"This is interesting but usually people are very grateful when they find flowers in their garden and when they receive them, so the cycle is often naturally completed by itself anyway. As you see there is not an epidemic of people being allergic to cut flowers, but the food products are starting to cause problems in many people."

When I am picking vegetables from my vegetable garden do I have to thank each plant individually or could I just thank all the vegetables all at once?

"Any way you feel guided is fine, it is the thankfulness energy directed back towards the plants that is important."

So this could be another reason why people are instinctively choosing to grow their own vegetables in their own backyards. They are better because of their freshness, being grown without chemicals and excessive transportation and they can be properly thanked there too. The thankfulness factor probably happens naturally anyway when someone picks a bountiful crop of vegetables from their own garden, they almost always feel properly pleased and grateful!

"Exactly, on a very large farm the farmer may use a large tractor and be tired and just pull in the crop without being that happy about it, particularly if he doesn't get enough money for it from the supermarkets. Or a farmer may hire cheap labour to harvest his crop and they may be resentful of the low price they are being paid. This energy then in turn is passed on to the people consuming his food."

"When bulk food is produced for very large manufacturers like a large bread company, good energy grain is mixed with bad energy grain from different farms so the whole process of having good energy bread is made more difficult because there are so many diverse players from many diverse circumstances adding their energy to the communal pot, so to speak."

"A small manufacturer who buys and grinds grain from one supplier say a family farm and then produces bread straight from that produces a superior product because they know the players and who they have bought the product from. In this way there is a distinct advantage to keeping production systems small and local. By keeping production systems small and local you get to control the energy purity of your product a little more."

Do we have to be thankful for everything, say the shade from a tree etc.? Would we not have much time to do other things if we ran around being grateful for everything?

"No you only need to be thankful for things that you are not truly thankful for, any falseness, on your behalf would be patently obvious and wouldn't benefit you or the plant anyway. However, thankfulness would be a good state to spend much of your life in, a permanent state of gratefulness for all you are receiving and experiencing anyway."

Yes, I suppose it would be. Like permanent state of grace, being conscious of all your blessings and in a permanent joyful high for all of life's blessings.

Baby Plants

I asked the gum trees whether there is a difference if I speak to very young baby plants to speaking to older more experienced plants? Is it worth talking to very small baby ones?

"Yes of course all communication is good and sometimes it is more valuable asking what the baby plants need in order to grow into big plants. The value of the communication is the same as you aren't strictly talking to the plants so much as the plants spirit and that spirit could be very wise. Small seedlings have lots of things to talk about. The information you get will not be inaccurate in any way, it will be the same."

Great. Gum trees, do plants lie to us at any time?

"No not really, they are not built to lie, what would that purpose be? There would be no point, plants like to love, not lie to people."

So you are able to communicate with any other plants in our garden?

"We are able to communicate with any plants in the region and others around the world if we so desire."

Do you usually talk to far away plants of different species from you?

"Yes, we do mainly via music, vibrations and humming. We talked to them via your human language for you because of your request to do so."

Do you mainly talk to fellow gum trees or all the plants?

"We talk to all the plants and can tune into the songs any variety we would like to hear from."

So do you have a special plant language?

"Yes and no, it is not a language so much as a line of communication. Every plant sings in a different way but to communicate between species we can communicate via telepathy mind pictures and the like."

I see. So if you were just talking to a gum tree of your particular species would you just sing and vibrate or would you use telepathy too?

"Both, we are as multi-dimensional as you humans are and can communicate in many different ways."

Do you do it for need, or for fun?

"Both sometimes we have a question to ask and other times we just want to socialize."

One more question, do you prefer to communicate telepathically via images and pictures or human words and sentences?

"Any really whatever will convey the message most clearly and concisely, sometimes that is word and sometimes pictures. We are equally proficient in either form of communication and have no preference."

I asked the gum trees how I can tell when one is getting telepathic messages and one is just imagining it?

"Telepathic messages come out of the blue and are clear images, have a clarity to them. Imagination rambles from subject to subject making up a story."

Circadian Rhythms

The sweet circle of life keeps on turning.

I asked the roses when they were going to put on their main flower show? They seemed quite a lot later this year compared to other years.

"From October 30 to November 30, we are flowering when we're meant to be, it is governed by the weather and the circadian rhythms. All is well. Start asking people to the rose garden from October 26 to November 15 for peak flowering enjoyment."

Arcadian rhythms?

"No circadian rhythms."

Thanks. What are circadian rhythms?

"The rhythmic cycles of all the planets, tides and planetary energies that go into determining the climate. In different cycles there are different patterns. We have just entered a completely new cycle, the first one for thousands of years, so expect great changes. It will be small and slow ones at first and then whole systems and climate zones are about to change dramatically."

"Your zone will change to one to more of your liking; you will get more cloudy days and more rain and humidity. Great for roses except for a little fungus here and there but better for continual flowering. It will get closer to the climate of inland China, where the roses came from in the first place. There will be a ten-year

change over period and then the climate will shift for their next period and then the climate will shift for their next semi-permanent cycle - at least it will last for a thousand years maybe more."

Can you tell me was climate change caused by us humans or was it meant to happen anyway?

"It was meant to happen and you have caused it and are causing it, so the answer is both. The new cycle will be more conducive to gardening and growing crops and plants and forests, giving the rainforests a chance of regenerating. Overall the dramatic changes will affect the whole world, nothing will remain exactly the same, no place will be spared the change, but the change is all good in the long run, you humans just need to accept and ride with the changes and have faith that they are all turning out for the best and for you benefit in the long run. If you all stay calm and peaceful, happy and in faith there will be no harm coming to you it is as simple as that. If you over-react and worry and think the worst of dramatic weather reports and this can affect the weather adversely. It is all conscious, the weather is listening to you all and is now directly taking its cues from you humans, you are the full controllers of your climate and your world, it is your responsibility to stay in calm and at peace and in joy and that is what the weather will give to you. You are becoming full controllers of your world in a way that you have never been before. The news is all good, but you will no longer be able to operate in the same old ways to the same old problems, you must learn new and enlightened ways of dealing and interacting with nature and your world around you."

So how will the rest of Australia cope with these changes?

"Very very well, as a rule you're optimistic, easy-going and enlightened community attitudes will bode well for smooth transition from one system to the next. Australia will get hotter and wetter in parts and cooler and moister in others. Mountain terrain will become cooler and moister and plains will become warmer and wetter, more tropical-temperate. The great inner centre of Australia will receive the most changes where it will fill up with water in the low-lying areas and the rain will provide massive new growth of trees and forests. This is the way it should be; the heart of Australia is its sacred heart and it will become great place of pilgrimage for its natural beauties, of wildflowers, flora and fauna in new heights, everything will hum and sing to the glory of God, humanity and Gaia it will be a great time for the world all will be well in the end, sit tight and enjoy the ride."

And the rest of the world?

"It is too numerous the changes to mention all here but suffice to say the changes are all good. They will be dramatic, but all good, people will still be able to live comfortably and prosperously on all the continents of the world plus a few more that either don't exist or aren't populated at the moment. There will be plenty of room for all and plenty of fertile land for food crops and great great gardens. The changes will be a complete surprise to all and for some countries a complete turn-around to what they have been living in but it is all for the best. The earth is gearing up for a new golden age and she want all her systems to come back to normal after being dormant for many thousands of years."

I asked the gum trees what is the best way to communicate with the nature angels?

"'By appreciation of the garden and nature and taking great care of it both on a local and global scale will put you all in the nature angel's good books. They love people caring for the environment big and small."

"'Being thankful for the world the angels do, they will feel the thankfulness and send you blessings.'"

"'By caring for your pets and farm animals with kindness and gentleness and love. Also caring for the plants, ground, rocks, mountains hills, sand dunes, rivers, lakes, streams swamps, deltas, sea and air. As you look after these things and eliminate pollution as much as possible, this communicates a love of the earth that vibrates in unison with all nature angels whatever the realm. Love your earth and it will love you right back.'"

Chapter 8
Fairy Questions

The curious heart will find what it seeks.

I asked the gum trees; What is the role of fairies in the garden and on earth?

"They are nature's caretakers and regulators, implementers and catalysts. They do these roles in varied ways shapes and forms according to their type and area of specialty."

Do different fairies within the same particular species have different roles or jobs or specialties?

"Yes, they are all individual with their own personalities, egos and levels of spiritual enlightenment and age."

Do fairies have different personalities?

"Yes, they all have their own personalities and likes and dislikes like humans."

Are they aware of us and can they read our minds and motives like plants?

"Yes of course, because we are all joined everything can really read another's mind, so-to-speak."

Do they ever come into our houses, are there some that live in houses?

"Yes, there are some they might come to clear the energy in a house and do some other form of work. Some are assigned to a particular piece of land and if a house happens to be built there, they may go the house too, but it is for the resident's benefit. They are very beneficial to have in the house or garden. They are beings of love and bring great blessings if they visit, reside in or are near a house."

"They are angels, angels of nature and there is no reason why you wouldn't want a visit from an angel?"

Yes, I see good point. Does it feel good when there are lots of fairies out in your garden tending to it?

"Yes, there is a noticeable, palpable feeling of their presence that is unlike any other. It feels good and exhilarating and exciting. That is why you always feel better in gardens there are rich in abundance and full of flowers or in natural forests and scrubland. It is the presence of the nature angels that heightens the frequencies of the area and makes if feel so much more refreshing, powerful and calming."

Do the plants feel like this too?

"Yes, we love the beneficial effects of the fairy presence and feel calm quiet and serene in their presence."

How do we humans know they are present?

"They are almost always present if you go out in a garden or outside. An overall feeling of wellbeing would be a good indication that fairies are present."

Do they ever have a role in looking after human beings?

"Yes, they have roles to look after and clear all of nature and sometimes this includes humans. They like to lift heavy and moods from people, clearing them so they can be open to feel more peace, joy and happiness. That is why it is so beneficial if you are in a bad mood to go outside and sit there for a while. You bad mood seems to evaporate. This does not happen by itself it was the kindly work of the fairies that made you feel much better."

Do fairies like our gardens?

"Of course fairies like it when humans go outside and tend nature. They just don't like it when humans spray poisons onto plants or insects outside. It can kill them or make them very sick. They are very sensitive to man-made chemicals and wished we wouldn't use them at all. The other ways of fertilizing and weeding gardens are more sustainable and healthier and fun for us in the long run anyway."

Do fairies stay up all night and spend time in our gardens doing work?

"No they spend the early evening and mornings working, then they get a little sleep and the rest of the time they play, sing, dance and the like."

Do fairies have favourite plants?

"Some do, some work specifically on one genus and species, others work between species doing general work. When at play they show their preferences for different plants leaves, herbs and flowers. They love the natural world and make things out of flowers and leaves and wood as well and decorating with flowers and leaves etc."

THE YEAR OF TALKING TO PLANTS: THE PLANTS AND FAIRIES TALK IN THEIR OWN WORDS

Do the fairies choose what varieties of seed to sow in the garden and do they help pollinate plants?

"Yes, to both questions. The fairies' roles is vast and never-ending in the garden. From a plant's inception to its eventual death and decomposition. Some sort of nature angel has a role in each stage of a plant's life. From the pollination of one variety to another, to which seed to choose and sow, to its early infancy, adulthood and maturity an old age. Nature angels are garden and nature's custodians and as such take great pride in their work and their ability to help each and every part of nature thrive."

"There are often conscious decisions as to which seed to plant, they know in advance how it will turn out, which are the superior varieties for flower and colour, and the best and tastiest fruit and vegetables etc. They often obtain advice from their elders about variety and species selection. There is often great thought that goes into what appears like random bush regeneration and plants self-sowing in your garden. There is no chance or coincidence in nature, just that same as with life. Everything is carefully planned and orchestrated to be of benefit to the rest of nature, it's habitats and the humans who reside in those habitats."

Do the fairies sow plants for humans because they know and like them? I am thinking about the petunias that have self-sown in my front garden pots. It was around that period I realized that I didn't have time to sow petunias for spring? I was disappointed until I saw these baby seedlings emerging triumphantly, out from the old plant remains.

"Yes of course they knew you wanted more of those particular-coloured petunias this year so they made sure ample were sown and came up. Do you like them?"

I love them, thanks very much! Can we ask the nature angels to not sow weeds in our garden?

"Yes, you can ask anything, but as to whether you will get it is something else. The fairies are not beholden to anyone, humans do not have power over them whatsoever, and whatever a human can offer them, they can easily obtain for themselves anyway, so wealth privilege, fame and attention mean nothing to them. What does mean something to them, however, is a kind human who shows kindness to animals and to the insects and the plants and environment, the fairies will bend over backwards to help these people and will grant them certain favours. They will not rearrange the whole of nature for them, but they can teach them, their magical ways and teach them to live more in love and peace and gentleness."

So if for instance I wanted the fairies to stop sowing grass weed on my gravel paths, would they oblige or is it beyond their jurisdiction?

"It is a little beyond them, there is not one group of nature angels there are many groups: many with overlapping interests. One wants more plants to aerate the ground and the other wants more for food for the bees and others want flowers for colour and so forth. So one fairy may stop sowing his particular weed on your path, but hundreds of others will take his place to help pollinate that spot with useful plants."

Is it against nature to have so many concrete paths and fake grass that some people are putting in their gardens these days?

"Yes and no, they understand the human's needs to have paths to comfortably get from A to B, but too much concrete and paving and fake grass is beyond the pale and against natures rules."

What do the fairies think of genetic modification and genetically engineered plants and crops?

"Need you even ask? The fairies greatly dislike such practices they go against nature's laws, the fairies' laws and Gods laws for nature. Everything has been perfectly set up; every human's need has been supplied on the planet. There is no more need for altered crops than there is to obtain another head. The fairies are nature's magicians and plant selectors and it is they who should be consulted if superior seed and crop varieties are sought, but the human way of obtaining it is wrong and can really put a lot of nature out of sync. When it becomes obvious to the general human population that fairies do indeed exist all of that silly manipulation will stop and the true world of cooperation with all of nature's systems will start."

Why do we need fairies in the environment when we have birds, animals and insects that seem to do similar things, what is the difference between fairies and insects?

"Insects do not think for themselves, they are followers and function mainly on instinct. Fairies on the other hand have individual minds, thought processes and personalities, so their role is of super-efficient gardeners and nature magicians. Remember they broach both this dimension and others so they get their wisdom and know-how from broad areas and they are capable of miracles in the garden. Insects in the other hand pollinate, procreate and eat. That is their role, they are nature little machines that keep each other in balance and clean and pollinate.

THE YEAR OF TALKING TO PLANTS: THE PLANTS AND FAIRIES TALK IN THEIR OWN WORDS

Fairies think and garden and decide on planting schemes, they sing and dance and have parties and celebrations they are more human than insect, they are really a sort of cross between a human and angel and their role is specifically to protect and uphold all of nature's systems."

Rain and Birdsong

It has been a glorious overcast day with the slightest hint that we may get some more rain. Roses, what did you think of the rain we received? Did you know we were going to receive it when we did and so heavily?

"Yes, we knew what and when. We prepared ourselves for it and rejoiced in it when it came, God provides for all your needs, you do not have to stress and strain for it, just ask and you shall receive it. Say it out loud if you want but just state and make clear what you next desire in the most relaxed way possible and then drop the subject completely. Just sit back and let the Universe unfold its blessings for you. You all deserve it so much. We plants watch you humans stressing and straining to get what you want without realizing that this stress chases away exactly what you desire. Sit back, kick off your shoes, think of what you want in as much detail as possible. Thank the Universe as though you have already received it and before you know it you will, when you least expect it in the most wonderful way. Your Universe is your mother, you can ask her for everything that you need on your journey through life and you will receive it, no questions asked. All is good, all is well, the Universe and we plants love you all."

Thank you. Roses, do you enjoy butterflies coming to you?

"Yes, it tickles. We enjoy quite a lot being pollinated; it feels quite sexual in nature."

Do plants have orgasms?

"Yes and no. Yes, we feel very much pleasure when we are pollinated but no it is not an orgasm like humans and animals have."

So animals have orgasms?

"Yes of course or they would not procreate, would they? Nor would many humans I suspect."

So what other times do plants feel pleasure?

"Almost all the time, we live permanently in a state of joy and bliss. We do not have problems like humans, that is not our role. Our role is support players to you the starring attractions. We do not have such a range of emotions and life experiences that you do, nor do we want to. We are content and simply blissful just doing what we are doing. Sitting and growing and being admired. That is what we love most of all."

Thriving in a State of Admiration

Does a rose bush grow better if it is admired on a regular basis by its owners compared to one that simply exists without attention from its human owners?

"Yes, interesting question. A rose bush that is shown admiration and attention on a regular basis simply thrives, even if it is given limited resources by way of food and water. It can bloom and bloom and really enjoy itself. "

"A bush that simply exists without attention from its human owners needs more resources to equal the blooming of his counterpart. It neither flowers as well or for as long and can be more susceptible to disease. Admired bushes get less disease whether it is roses or other plants. All plants exist in a state of bliss even if they live somewhere devoid of humans, like in some hidden valley somewhere uninhabited. However, the ones that have human contact and admiration and even admiration from animals thrive on such positive attention and vibes. It literally gives them extra love nutrients that can sustain them for longer.'

Do plants in public places like parks that get admiration from people benefit from that attention?

"Of course all thankfulness and admiration for us counts whether it is from people driving by in cars or from an owner working in his garden."

Is birdsong beneficial to the plants and fairies too as well as humans?

"Birdsong is a vital musical element in nature. They hit the right tones that vibrate through the whole of nature spreading love and nurturing energy whenever it is heard. To hear live birdsong is an extremely healing thing to do. Birdsong is one element of fairies' music; the birds often sing when the fairies tell them to."

Ooh nice one! Do birds and animals see fairies?

"Yes and no. Birds mostly do, some don't. Cats and dogs don't but many wild animals do or at least can sense them with their more sensitive natural instincts.'

'Hearing live birdsong is a magical healing tool; people could sit outside every day to absorb the beneficial tones and tunes from birds. Just five minutes of sitting amongst the birdsong can equal a half hour session of yoga session as far as its healing and calming actually goes. Birdsong is yoga for the senses."

Why does it have to be live birdsong can't it be recorded?

"No, it must be live music straight from the birds for maximum benefit. The same as gentle live music is more beneficial to humans than CD music. Although CD music is highly preferable to none at all. It's all a matter of degrees of effectiveness.'

'Birdsong, frog croaks, cricket chirping, cicada humming it is all very healing to the senses. Go outside into nature today even for five minutes to soak up the tunes from your local wildlife, your soul will thank you for it."

What about humans singing or humming tunes?

"This is also as effective healing device both for the person singing and for the listeners. The tunes and musical vibrations, reverberate around the universe that is how important music is."

Does any sound suffice? What about clanging saucepans and purring car engines?

"No, if they feel slightly stressful, discordant, annoying or loud then the noise is noise pollution and not beneficial to the human soul. It detracts from the living experience instead of enhancing it. Sound is variable and must be sweet, tuneful and melodic to be of benefit to all on the earth and nature."

What happens if someone sings out of tune?

"Any singing is good and of benefit unless it is screaming obscenities. Even if it is off-key, it enhances life for both the singer and the audience."

So if the singer intends to sing a tune it is good no matter what the result?

"The sweeter it is the better it is for you. A highly trained or a person who sings particularly from the heart are the best people to listen to but an out-of-tune husband or wife's songs are also of some benefit. Singing is often a release of excess pent-up emotions and feelings. It can also provoke a release of pent-up feeling in an audience which is beneficial but that is just the start. Music has a lot more depth than that. It can achieve amazing things but that is a story for another day."

Little Urges Leading Us to Missing Objects

Gum trees does normal praying over our food before we eat suffice for being thankful to the plants?

"Any prayers of thanks are good but they are incomplete and disrespectful without including the original source of your food which was the plant and then *there is the rain and the clouds, the country, Gaia and God. But to thank the plant creates a direct link of thankfulness which includes the plants in your blessings otherwise they get somewhat left out of the equation."*

Gum trees do you know what ley lines are?

"They are energy grids that traverse the planet from North to South Pole, equator to equator. They transmit energy down the lines that can hasten learning, travel and dimensional travel. They are like information super-highways, if you like but this time this is the Universal super-highway not the earth computer one."

Are there good and bad fairies like some of the fairy tales suggest? Can a person be misled by fairies?

"No not really, you could be misled in as much as they behave in a way that reflects you. If you are a deceptive sort of person, then you might find deception in other aspects of your life like people and situations etc."

"There are no good and bad fairies. This is a complete fabrication in the minds of humans. It makes for a good and dramatic storyline but that is all it is, a fable. Fairies are all about loving and caring for nature, plants, rocks, wind and sea; they are about maintaining, nurturing, having fun and living with joy. They are not about destroying other people's fun or doing evil acts. This is counter-productive to the reason why they are on earth, to maintain, love and nurture. It's like saying do mothers do evil things, well some might but the vast majority do not, as their role also is to nurture, maintain and love."

To find something lost is to realize that it was never gone forever. It was just put aside by God for safe-keeping!

A funny idea came to me today. I had been walking through an area and had the sudden urge to take cuttings of pelargonium using the pots I had that were sitting under a climbing rose plant. I stopped what I was doing and went there. As I was filling up the pot with potting mix there, I was bending down and saw a missing pair of secateurs. There is no way I would have found them in my normal course of affairs, had I not been bobbing down in that position. It was only then that I wondered if I had been led to that position deliberately. It is not the first time that I have happened upon a missing object in this way, having a sudden urge to go to an out-of-the-way place.

Climbing rose plant, can you tell me if I was deliberately led to my secateurs and if so by whom?

"Well it was me and my fairy; we wanted you to find the tool and had to make up a reason for you to go in such a spot this end of the week. You have been without them for more than a week and we thought you could use them."

Thank you so much rose bush; this is very much appreciated! Do you know whether other plants and fairies have helped me in this way and does this commonly happen to other gardeners and people who work closely out in nature?

"Yes, this happens to you all the time, like you suddenly realize that your sudden urge to do something out of the normal and then finding a missing object or seeing a fruit or lovely flower is nature's way of rewarding those they love. This commonly happens to all keen gardeners and people who love nature. Nature the plants, rocks and angels and fairies will conspire from time to time to do these people special favours or treats."

This is a really delightful idea. It is a phenomenon that I didn't really notice consciously before. I will have to be more aware as I work around the garden in the future. I would have to admit that I am often misplacing my garden tools, as many gardeners do.

I asked the tomatoes if there is any value in planting by the moon?

"Yes and no, when planting seed it is good to notice the moon phases. However, in general it is better to plant seeds and plant by the correct season on overcast days, when the days are at their coolest. To keep them watered well for four to eight weeks minimum for establishment. To plants seeds in pots in shady areas or in the ground with some sort of covering in hot regions and glass in cool areas. The list goes on so the moon phases can be beneficial for seeds but for plants the effect would be minimal because they are already operating with the moon phases as they sit in the pots anyway. Whereas when you choose some new seed, this is not activated until you plant it."

So even with seed planting other factors are more important such as regular watering etc.?

"Yes of course, proper tending and care always supersedes any other thing you can do for a plant regardless of where or when you plant it. You can grow plants in the desert if you desire, you just need to know how to tend it in order to thrive."

The Mystery of My Tasmanian Visits Explained

Gum trees I don't know whether you have an answer to this but what was I feeling in Tasmania on my first trip in particular? Why did I feel the trees were telling me to go away?

"Yes, Tasmania is an 'Isle of Healing' not only on a personal level but also a local scale and a global one too. You were feeling and hearing the forest's combined message for all the people who want to harm the trees and forests to go away. It was a general cry for help and not a personal one, as you may have surmised."

"Tasmania is a sacred healing island built on the axis of a few sacred grids. These grids give power to the island's healing abilities but it needs its tree and fairy communities and forests intact to perform their sacred deeds."

"Tasmania is the Southern hemispheres cleaning device; it cleans the air and atmosphere and the sea around it. Its significance is more for the environment as a whole rather than personal but people who are in great need of physical and mental and particularly emotional healing are drawn to the island and it sends out its healing energy to them."

"The island likes to be inhabited by people as long as they are sensitive to the environment and respectful of the trees, shrubs, plants and forest communities. People who like and respect trees are welcome. The whole island is a temperate rainforest with mystical qualities. Psychics are both drawn and repelled by the place because it can increase their psychic abilities, which depending on their preferences are either favourable or unfavourable. This is only a temporary experience when the person stays on the island. Tasmania beams out good vibrations and positive frequencies to the world from its forests and from deep below the forests."

Where is the Northern hemispheres healing place?

"Great Britain and Ireland."

Does this act like Tasmania?

"*Yes and no, because of the greatly changed landscape around them their healing energies is not as pure and pristine as Tasmania's, which is more effective in maintaining the purity of the region. Nevertheless, as the grids are activated again and as the human systems are activated again the true nature of these healing islands will be revealed and hidden areas will be able to be tapped into for personal healing.*"

So gum trees, is Tasmania good to visit and live, just so long as you respect the environment and forests there?

"*Exactly that is the only message that the trees were sending out.*"

Ok thanks. Wow that was interesting.

There are no mysteries in life, just a question that has yet to be asked.

Chapter 9
Plants Speaking Only if Spoken To.

What if I knew what nature thought? I would have a direct line to Mother Earth herself!

When considering telepathic communication with plants previously, I thought it may be very confusing with many voices of different plants talking to you whenever you go outside. However, this is far from the truth. What in fact happens is that they never talk telepathically to you unless you first address them. In other words, they only speak if they are spoken to. So that way you are not confused by a plethora of sound and mental images all at once from the millions of plants that reside outside.

This keeps things simple, calm and to the point. If you want to talk to a plant, you can and if you do not, you can go about your business as per usual. I dare say the same thing happens with communication between other species such as rocks, and animals.

Gum trees has there been in the last few years a thinning of the veil so-to-speak, has it been easier for humanity (and me) to speak to plants that earlier?

"Yes, in the last two years there has been a lightening of your (human) energy so it is easier to detect life and consciousness in other things on the planet. There is no mistake that at the same time your (humanities) awareness of entities like the loving angels and guides has also increased we are all becoming aware of what was always there but was once unseen. Now humanity is starting to become more sensitive to finer frequencies and finer signals."

A mood in a tree is like a rainbow with a frown.

Do trees have moods?

"Yes, but it is one mood, mainly one of peace, happiness and joy. Sometimes we can be in distress if one of us or any animal or person is harmed, but on the whole, we reside in the eternal peace that is available to all."

Hollyhocks do some plants like being in the company of certain plants and not others?

"Definitely it depends which are the plants that would naturally fit into their indigenous plant climate zone map. We prefer plants that can grow in similar regions. We don't get along so well with plants that have say different water, soil or room needs as need more or less light than others. We vibrate well with plants from similar areas of the world. Not really plants from the same country or area although that is nice but ones with similar needs to ours, that are not hogging the others plant space, sun, water, nutrients etc. Within this issue there are plants that are complimentary to others that lend themselves to growing with each other. Especially if there is something that they need like an oak tree giving nutrients to a crop of mushrooms underneath them or garlic and chives with roses etc."

With the preparation for Christmas and shopping and entertaining I have not been doing much gardening lately. Gum trees, do plants have celebrations?

"Yes, we celebrate everyday with our joy for life and love. We think of every day as a cause for a celebration, you never need a reason for a party or get together. Life is to be savoured and enjoyed, no suffered through."

Do the fairies celebrate?

"They like to celebrate even more than we do. Almost nightly the fairies hold some sort of party or another. They love to sing and dance, drink, eat, tell stories and jokes. Very much like humans, only smaller!"

Cute! Do fairies celebrate say around Christmas too?

"No not really that is more a human thing although those that live close to humans join in the frivolity and the love the decoration and joy. Fairies celebrate special occasions, birthdays, season changes, the equinoxes etc. They even have

*full and new moon celebrations. They celebrate the harvest, the summertime, the
winter lushness and the autumn colours. They celebrate when one of them their
midst has achieved a big goal say a celebration or a victory in the job they do or
when the humans finally start clearing up the environment around them or they
have attained a new goal in their spiritual quests."*

Fairy Self-Sown Seed Magic

Dear tomato plant: (I am addressing a self-sown tomato that is growing in
one of my pots) Why do plants that are self-sown grow so much better and
quicker than the ones that human's plant?

*"This is because they are chosen by the fairies to particularly grow there, they
perform some of their magic just for good measure to make sure they grow really
well. Why else do you think weeds grow so well and so vigorously? Also they are
grown at the exact right time, by the exact right seed chosen for its vigour. It is not
a random process; it is planned from start to finish. Do you like me? I was grown
especially for you since you like tomatoes so much?"*

Yes, I do thank you very much!

Overcast skies, but a smile in my heart.

Today is a deliciously overcast day where all the colours seem brighter and
the greens seem greener. The flowers look like little jewels against the green
backdrop. The butterflies are fluttering around the garden en-masse creating
liveliness and delight. A little like I would imagine the fairies would look like
flying around the garden. On our top hill a small group of rainbow bee-eater
birds are tooting away and joyously swooping from tree to tree, supping on an
aerial feast of insects that frequent the spring skies. Spring is so lovely and so
busy. Everything comes alive and sings the dance of life's joy.

Gum trees do the fairies sow seeds in colour schemes? Do they colour-coordinate?

"I would say yes, they do, they are telling me they like to choose colours that are bright and happy and that they like unusual colour combinations and go for these when they make planting decisions. Also the site may call for more red or orange to add different elements to the landscape of passion and creativity. The surrounding plants may need more flowers of that colour to maintain their good health. Colour decisions are not simply made for aesthetics reasons alone."

Does one fairy choose or is it a team?

"They are almost always team workers and consult and make decisions as a group or even as a pair. You seldom see only one fairy working alone usually they work in family and societal groups according to their particular role in the landscape."

Do fairies have their own gardens?

"They consider whatever they are working on at the time is their garden but they do plant favourite plants near their home bases. They don't have ownership issues in the same way that humans do."

Fairies live in a place of here that is nowhere, and yet somewhere at the same time.

Where is a fairy's home? What do they consist of?

"Fairies and other nature angels home bases are often inter-dimensional in that they are partly here in this dimension such as under a rock but they are then partly in another dimension when they built caverns under the rock to form a home with rooms. There are whole cities of fairy home bases at regular intervals throughout the landscapes and seascapes all around the world. Some are under the earth, some are found in logs, under the sea etc."

Do they have separate familial houses like us?

"Yes, most do but some have very large families and the houses have many rooms for all the family members and big rooms to house large gatherings of them, their houses are as individual as yours are."

Do fairies have furniture and possessions?

"Yes, they do, some don't but most like to have things that they call their own. Fairies are masters of manifestation and can manifest what they want just by thinking about it, they can imagine up furniture and objects in and as many varieties as they like and when they get tired of them, they just imagine them out

of existence. In their dimensions there is no competition for resources or wealth or land because there is plenty for all. There is no competition for resources in your dimension either but many of you are not aware of it as yet."

Do fairies have favourite things that we humans can put in our gardens?

"Their favourite things are mixed plantings, planted in profusion and very closely. They like hidden nooks and crannies in a garden or park. They like plants with flowers and with scents. They also like water features of any kind and havens for wildlife. They also like ornamentation such as garden lights, statues and other decorations. They think they are fun and like humans that have a sense of humour in their statuary and decoration. Informal planting and cottagey wild style landscapes are preferred to formal clipped and primped gardens. Fairies will not go to places that are sprayed with chemicals or use too much chemical fertilizers."

Do fairies have families like us?

"Yes, the do like humans, except kinder and more caring and the families are larger and more communal where jobs and child rearing are shared."

Do fairies have names?

"Yes, they have names just like humans and they also sometimes have surnames but they are more nature based such as Airsylf Root-dweller. Fairies tend to mainly mix in they own group and communities so most times one individual name is all that is required for everyone to know who it is. Fairies do not tend to repeat the same name like humans do, like John and Mary. Many times they like to make up new manes in honour of their new babies."

Do fairies have hobbies and jobs like us?

"Yes, they love music, singing art and crafts of many different sorts they like to play and dance. Many fairies and gnomes have different personal hobbies to their jobs, but mainly they 'play' at their jobs so there is no need to seek interest elsewhere. Every fairy loves their main job which is more like a life-purpose than a job."

Photo Orbs

That secret spiritual place is a secret no more with orbs announcing spirit's presence.

I absolutely adore taking photographs of my garden and all the beautiful flowers of each season. I use photographs as an enhancement of my experience of gardening. It informs me of the change of seasons, the complexity of the flowers and forms. It helps me keep a record of the planting schemes that I use in a particular year, so that I can repeat them or improve on them if I feel the need. It is a fun way of participating in the garden. Recently there have been quite a few coloured orbs in photos I have of people.

Gum trees can you tell me what they are?

"Yes, they are the angels, guides and other spiritual helpers that guide, protect and send love to humans, animals and plants. We all have them, but with the new precise digital photography it is starting to pick up these entities particularly in the early mornings and evenings when the light is soft and diffuse."

Yes, that is when these orbs have occurred in the photos, do you think there will be a time when we will see these orbs with our naked eyes?

"I can do one better, there will be a time when all humans will be able to see the shapes and faces of these entities and clearly see who they are and will be able to communicate with them freely, like I am doing with you. This time is in the not-too-distant future."

Gum trees are there special angels or fairies that you ask (as a tree), like archangels to accomplish tasks for you?

"Yes, there are numerous angels and nature angels that we can ask if we have a special request. We can ask our angel to petition others for help or ask the angels of place to consider our request. Say one is having problems with a human stripping his bark, he will ask the fairies/angels if they can persuade the human to stop. They will then contact the human's angels and see if they can pursue a better way of operating. Their angel will implant ideas into the human's consciousness and give them ideas of other ways of operating. The humans then can decide to adhere to or ignore the advice, it is up to them, as this is a planet of free will."

It is that glorious time of evening when the sun goes down making the gum trees foliage twinkle little sparkles of light in the waning sun. There is a fine suspension of dust in the air, giving a dream-like quality to the hills on the edge of our little valley. Everything shimmers and glows. Colourful flower petals turn luminescent as the sunlight shines through them like miniature-stained glass windows. The colours of the flowers seem somehow brighter and more intense in the fading sun of dusk. Evening is a glorious time.

Orange tree why have you looked so sick lately?

"Two things, one is the rain isn't as regular as it used to be from the downpipe. Secondly, I don't like even the smell of the water that you've been putting on the lemon tree for your washing water. I don't like that laundry powder. "

Lemon tree, do you like the washing water we are giving you?

"Yes, I like it better than not getting any water at all but would prefer a cleaner water source."

What sort of washing powder should I use?

"One with less detergents, try this mixture:"

The Lemon Tree's Washing Paste Recipe

1 part pure soap flakes

2 parts baking soda

1 teaspoon eucalyptus oil

Dissolve in some warm water to make a wet paste then put in washing machine.

🦋 🦋 🦋

Gum trees do fairies faces and bodies look a particular way? Do they look like children's fairy book drawings? Or is it our expectations that is leading the way in the appearance stakes?

"Yes, interesting question, we can't say what they look like, they feel a certain way to us. What they look like to you is up to you. We cannot tell. The fairies tell me that their looks are based on people's perceptions of them but the reality is not too far from the truth. Anyway it is more important that people know of their existence and love them than to quibble over their appearance."

Quite true. Do fairies come inside our houses much and if so for what reason?

"They come inside to help improve and cleanse the atmosphere of the home and occupants, fairies go in and out of people's houses. Some come in on gusts of wind, others walk through walls, some come in with the flower bunches on vegetables or fresh fruit. If fairies don't come in on the produce, then it is not worth eating because it is not fresh. Sometimes they come in via invitation of houses residents but this is rare and other times that is where they live. A home sometimes has a resident nature angel of one form or another."

How fascinating! How can we encourage fairies to come inside?

"By being calm and quiet and serene. By playing tuneful music and having fun. By bringing the outdoors in, in the form of flowers and fresh produce. By keeping indoor plants in the house. As each plant is accompanied by numerous fairies for its livelihood."

Is having indoor plants in the house good for us?

"It is good for humans and the atmosphere of the home, it guarantees its own supply of fresh air, air conditioning and air purifying. Electronic smog and indoor pollution from synthetic chemicals used in furniture etc. is neutralized with the more plants you have. Each room should have ideally at least five plants in it to keep it in optimum health. These plants could be alternated with others outside in a constant flow of fresh healthy greenery. Plants also mop-up emotional refuse that is left behind in the normal activities of the day. One would feel the atmosphere to be cleaner and easier to concentrate in."

Ooh lovely! Can humans have more control of the elements such as the wind, rain, hail etc.

"Yes of course in a few years' time many of you will regain some of your knowledge of how to summon and work with the elements, in one joyous tandem

movement. But for now it is not as important as keeping positive mindsets and being grateful and happy for what you have now. Love the situation you are in and it will transform your next moment."

Gum trees, do the fairies mind if we choose our own plants and colours for the garden?

"No not at all the gardens are there primarily for human use learning and enjoyment, the fairies just maintain them and the greater part of nature to make sure it is all self-sustaining."

What if we pull out things they have planted, like the weeds?

"Yes, they don't mind at all. The lifecycle of a plant is only meant to be a short time to help rejuvenate the soil and to bring greenery to the landscape. Like a green manure crop that is grown and turned into the soil before it seeds to bulk up the humus content of the soil."

Trees Seeing Auras

A tree is more than a mere collection of leaves and roots, it is a spiritual presence, an entity of importance grounding Mother Earths desire for safety and comfort for us.

I can't help it, gazing upon a garden full of flowers fills me with absolute joy! I enjoy giving flower bunches, little plants grown in my garden and food made from its produce. Lemon balm what are the benefits to humans of giving produce from the garden to others, apart from the obvious nutritional ones?

"Yes, produce picked fresh from the garden still has the energy of life and fairies upon it. These bring many blessings to the person receiving it and their house; the house will start to feel fresher and cleaner and more vital and alive. The residents will start to smile for no reason and be less likely to pick arguments with each other and *feel suddenly inspired and happy. It is a blessed house that receives gifts from nature."*

Lovely, I will think of that when I share garden produce from now on. Gum trees can you sense people auras? Do you know what colour mine is for instance?

"Yes, we can that is the main way we sense human beings, yours is bottle green, with deep blue, lilac, violet, yellow hands and a lot of baby pink."

What does that mean?

"It means that you have a life purpose in teaching and communicating blue, violet and lilac, and it will be communicating spiritual and higher learning concepts. The baby pink is of motherhood and impending motherhood and of caring for your family as a personal life purpose. The yellow is your inquisitiveness and searching for the higher truth of situations in order to get the answers and truth of any given situation. This is what you are currently working on now. The blue is communicating and counselling people. The Bottle green or royal emerald green your overall colour and explains why you are so passionate about plants it shows a life purpose involving and surrounding yourself with nature and the nature angels. You also have a little gold and a spot of silver which speak of grasping some of the higher concepts of universal love and oneness."

Wow thank you, that was great, that wasn't going to be the question I was to ask you, I forgot that and instead thought of this one. Can all trees and plants see auras?

THE YEAR OF TALKING TO PLANTS: THE PLANTS AND FAIRIES TALK IN THEIR OWN WORDS

"Yes, and they know how to interpret them."

Do fairies see us as auras or do they see us with their seeing sight, with their eyes?

"They see both, a being humanoid in form they have all the attributes that humans have plus being part plant and part angel they also have the talent coming from these areas too so they are psychic and can clearly see auras with their eyes too."

Fabulous, thank you. How would I go about seeing fairies and how could the reader accomplish this?

"You would set the genuine intention of seeing them and releasing any preconceived ideas you have about how they will appear to you. It may be in your actual sight that you see them or with your spiritual sight, or in your imagination. You may see outlines at first or maybe little lights, that is the fairy lights. Psychic talent is a learned skill and comes upon a human gradually so at first one might see the occasional small light or glow or outlines of the nature beings."

Psychic talent is seeing with the eyes of God.

Would one feel confused and overwhelmed when seeing so many at work and does one see them all the time or just every now and then?

"You can see them only when you choose to see them or you can see them all the time it is entirely up to you or you cannot see them at all which is what most of humanities switch is set to because they don't believe they exist and there is also the fear of seeing them. There are many false myths perpetrated about fairies, trolls and goblins etc. Which by-the-way are complete falsehoods and are not true at all. They were all man-made to scare people from empowering themselves with the truth."

"Just because you can't see them doesn't mean they aren't there and going about their daily business every day from time immemorial."

"Fear is however the main obstacle to psychic sight of any kind. If you fear seeing something you just won't regardless of whether it is there or not."'

How does one release the fear of seeing fairies?

"One has to learn to trust them and trust your psychic sight. One has to start feeling love for these dear little beings who work for your behalf every day of your life. They are completely selfless and do what needs to be done, come rain, hail or shine. Their job is not to question but to serve the earth and nature and humans and animals and to love what they are doing, and do they love it!"

"One can also ask the fairies who are champion healers and magicians for them to take away your fear of seeing them. This would also be highly effective too. It is most important that humanity starts seeing the nature angels because it is only then that real communication and cooperation will start."

"It is hard to talk to something if you can't see it, like you have found."

So just because one starts seeing them one would not necessarily hear them all, do they make noise as they work?

"They make a lot of noise in their own dimension; you could turn up your psychic hearing too. Again this is by choice and one can learn to turn that off and on at will but that is a lesson for another day."

So can I talk to them like I am talking to you if I address one of them?

"Yes, exactly the same. You won't hear necessarily with your ears but with words or images or even ideas in your mind."

So you don't hear them, you just sense them and hear their vibrations?

"Exactly so."

How many people on earth do you think can talk to plants as I am now?

"Not that many yet but in a few years' time when the current children get a little bit older, they will amaze you all with their special talents. They will lead the way as people like you are, in bringing peace on earth and love and communication between all things."

Gum tree what do the fairies do when it gets hot in the middle of the day?

"They hide under the shade bushes and inside trees and under rocks or sleep in their homes. They are there but they are often in other dimensions of there."

So they don't go out in the midday sun?

"No not normally. They let the plants be and tend to them in the evening again."

Fairies of Place

Gum trees last night I had the urge late in the evening when I was about to go inside to water a young gum tree. When I walked in that direction with the watering can I walked toward the vegetable garden I remembered I had left the watering drippers on. I would not have remembered if I hadn't decided to water that tree. Was there plant, fairy or divine intervention there?

"Yes, it was the plant 'fairies of place' who look after your garden. They knew that you would not have been very happy if you had left the tap on, so they intervened whispering that perhaps it would be good to water that little gum tree before you go inside. These fairies are more the overlords of the area and look after the area in the vicinity of a two to ten-kilometre radius."

So what is their role and how many of them are there here?

"There are two sometimes three. Their job is to coordinate the troops so-to-speak and cope with any environmental or human changes to the landscape and to assign other nature angels to different places or to call on more if need be."

So are they aware of my writing work and my work in the garden?

"Of course they are. They lend a helping hand to you and anyone else who has nature's best interests at heart. Quite often, when you are gently reminded of something to do with the garden, it is coming primarily for them."

What are they officially called? *"Fairies or angels of place or fauns."*

What do they look like?

"They are much taller than the fairies and are sometimes the size of a small child or a little taller than a human depending on where they come from in the world and what their roles are. They are especially attentive to your needs, being a major messenger on behalf of the environment.'

Wow how fabulous! I thank them. How do they give such strong suggestions in your mind and does my guidance allow it?

"Yes, your guidance and angels are always looking out for your best interest, but when a message comes by that is in your environments best interest, they will let it through and you get to choose as to whether you act upon it or not. Your higher self only allows in what is for your highest and best interests."

Are they always there or do they go in and out of dimensions.

"They are always there in one form or another."

Can they change form?

"Yes, they can, if they need to reduce in size to look inside a log they can shrink or grow wings to fly high above the landscape, all in the service of being guardians of the landscape."

What wonderful beings they are. What do they guard, the rocks, plants or people?

"They guard the lot and make changes where necessary to keep everything in balance."

THE YEAR OF TALKING TO PLANTS: THE PLANTS AND FAIRIES TALK IN THEIR OWN WORDS

Chapter 10
Wise Plants

All plants are wise but some hold great knowledge far beyond their years and experience. These wise plants are the go-to plants for specific knowledge to specific questions.

Dear gum trees, does wood, dead wood all cut up hold any consciousness?

"Yes, it does in a way, everything is consciousness as you well know, wood like other objects holds memories of what it has experienced and who has owned it and touched it etc., that can be read by people who are sensitive to such things. There are certain wood that keep their healing properties long after the tree they came from has died such as oak, elm and certain conifers. There are others that can help elevate your thoughts etc. plus others that help to purity an atmosphere and still others that help elicit great wisdom, oak, eucalypt, beech, elm, coconut, cassia etc."

Are dried flowers good to have in the house, in feng shui they say they aren't?

"Yes, dried flowers are fine, especially if they are colourful fragrant and give you great joy. If you don't like them, then it's best not to have them."

Do they hold consciousness?

"Not the same as wood but they do in their own quiet way, if they smell the same as their fresh counterpart as with lavender then they bring great blessings to the household as do dried herbs, fruit, mushrooms, seeds etc."

Thanks, another question do the plants talk to the insects? This has come up several times.

"Yes, all the time that is how insects know how to go to certain flowers and not to others because they are vibrating at a certain rate that the insects can pick up on and they follow these vibrations to get their bearings and direction and the most succulent nectar or pollen."

When a plant says it is a wise plant what is that all about? When I was talking to the plants this has come up many times.

"A wise plant is one beloved of all ancient and modern nature medicine practitioners such as shamen and witch-doctors. They can ask these plants questions to medical questions of any sort and they will elicit a cure from nature complete with medicine recipes."

Oh that's clever. How have we lost such instincts?

"Well you haven't lost the instincts just the knowledge that you can get knowledgeable and reliable information from nature about any ailment.'

How exciting! Gum trees sometimes when I go outside if I am in a bad mood or upset, after a while I feel much more relaxed and peaceful. What is it in nature that causes such positive effects?

"Yes, it is the trees, the plants and the nature angels. If you go outside and you are feeling unbalanced the nature angels work hard to bring you back to your natural state of calmness and peace, which is every human's natural state. They do this by working with your aura and energy and removing any other person's or energies that are not yours and clearing you. This is part of what nature's systems do. Sometimes humans spend too much time indoors away from nature and its cleansing systems, which is where humans should spend the majority of their time. The outdoors has systems in place, to help keep humans at their optimum good health. Nature angels have systems in place to cleanse and clear any humans and animals that are out of balance. Nature aims for balance at all times."

Do seeds have consciousness in the same way you do?

"Yes, indeed they do, they can tell you all sorts of things. They will give you a picture of what sort of plant they are and what their flowers colour or fruit will be like."

Plant Reincarnation

Gum trees should we warn the fairies if we use the lawnmower or other tools to trim in the garden?

"Yes, that would be a good idea, sometimes they are quietly going about their own business oblivious to what the humans are doing as around them. It would be thoughtful to let them know either out loud or in your mind."

Weeds as Teachers

Gum trees what is the beneficial effects of leaving a few weeds in the garden whether it be the vegetable or flower garden?

"Weeds are a natural part of the living landscape; they are built to withstand all that an environment can dish out whether it be pests or weather extremes. Weeds have inherent built-in toughness; this tough ability and stamina and adaptability can be taught to the surrounding plants. Weeds can teach and persuade other plants what to do in order to survive and thrive in an area. Weeds can be valuable teachers and leaders via example of how to grow well and excel. If you eliminate all weeds and every example of weeds you eliminate whole encyclopedias of plant knowledge and experience that can be taught to other plants and humans. A garden is always better off with a few good-looking weeds included in it

Weeds perform the valuable task of renewal of the soil, the air and the atmosphere. If nature did not fill in the bare gaps in the soil, decay would soon result, pollution would build up, the soil would lose its fertility, the air would get thinner and less viable for human and animal habitation on the planet. The planet needs weeds like people need air, weeds contribute a lot to the very air we breathe. Without weeds there would be no life on earth, it is that simple."

He, he! I'll try to remember that! Do plants reincarnate?

"Yes of course they do, nothing ever ceases its existence, and in answer to your next question yes fairies and nature angels of every sort also reincarnate."

Do plants reincarnate as the same sort of plants or different ones or a fairy or an animal?

"As a general rule plants stick to their own species and plant variety; I might reincarnate as another sort of eucalypt or maybe a small native daisy bush to experience life closer to the earth. In other lives I have had, I've been an acacia, box thorn, a liverwort and numerous grasses but mainly a eucalypt. We do not incarnate as a fairy or an animal as a general rule although this can sometimes happen for another species to feel what it is like to be something else for a lifetime."

I see. But usually a eucalypt would keep on coming back as a eucalypt in the same country?

"Yes, if one enjoys it and did a good job there is no reason to really change things is there? We often let our over-souls or guides guide us to our next choice of incarnation, we trust that this is the best and highest decision on our behalf."

OK. Do animals reincarnate as plants?

"Not really as a rule, species like to stick to their own species."

So animals, plants, people and fairies reincarnate and rocks too?

"Yes, but the lifetime of a rock is a very very long one, but there is always a chance to be something else."

Are there some plants that don't like to talk or us or won't talk telepathically with humans?

"We find the small plants and bacteria difficult to talk to but apart from that if approached respectfully most other plants will give you the time of day, so-to-speak."

Do some plants refuse to speak?

"Some may, some may not talk to particular people if they view them as plant or nature haters. But these sorts of people wouldn't think to talk to a plant anyway!"

Yes, true. Would say a little petunia that has had a short life cycle reincarnate in the same garden in the next generation?

"Yes, that is exactly the sort of example that is most common. Over half the petunias that you have in pots this year are the same petunia souls that you had the year before. They loved it so much they came back to the same garden and even have their same pots."

How incredible I did not even give this a thought before!

"I know."

So this would be common with annuals in people's gardens?

"Yes indeed. They say you are looking after them better this time around but they enjoyed their last life with you nevertheless."

Oh that's very sweet. Yes, I'm watering them more regularly this year. So fairies reincarnate too like humans and plants?

"Yes."

Do some of them come back to the same garden again?

"Yes, they do, this is the most common way."

Do they retain their same knowledge for their last incarnation consciously?

"Yes, they do, they know of all that goes before, after they have grown into adult fairies it gradually comes back to them."

What is the average fairy lifespan?

"Some live to 300 to 600 years old, others only live 5 or 10 years. It depends on the fairy variety, specialty area etc. The ones that look after the rocks and waterways are the longest lived, then come the fairies that live in forests due to their ideal conditions. Ones that have closer contact with humans have shortened life spans due to the physical, emotional and mental pollution that they have contact with. But lives lived close to human beings bring with it more spiritual advancement and learning."

So a more difficult life but greater rewards?

"Yes, in a way, it's true."

What do you think are the main benefits of inter species communication like between plants and people?

"Well it would seem breaking down the barriers of ignorance would be the first reason. Once people realize that the whole earth and everything in it is conscious and intelligent and loving then this paves the way for peace on earth. When one can communicate with one's plants and animals and rocks you can do a better job in life, have a better garden, build a better house and live life more lovingly with the advantage of being able to speak to nature and the world around you. Everything under the sun will get better when people start communicating telepathically with plants and animals and even the fairies if they so wish. It is nature's dearest wish for all life on earth to talk and understand each other and have compassion for everyone's point of view. Quite simply inter-species communication is the best way to go about this."

Chapter 11
First Fairy Contact

That exciting moment of meeting a new friend who perhaps you knew before at some other time, at some other place.

Gum trees I wonder if you could help me to meet a nice plant fairy, introduce me so that I could talk directly to one maybe tomorrow?

"Yes, no problems tomorrow will be fine."

Gum trees, do trees communicate much with animals?

"Not so much although we can, we tend to talk more amongst ourselves, the nature angels and the insects. The animals go about their own business, we are glad they are there and we know what they are doing."

First Fairy Meeting
The following day.

Hello gums trees. Have you got a fairy for me to talk to?

"Yes."

What is his or her name?

"Gentica, she is a female over-fairy of the woods."

Good morning Gentica.

"Good morning, Sarah."

Are you an over-fairy in charge of my garden and surrounds?

"Yes, my region goes as far as the eye can see over all the surrounding hills."

The gum tree mentioned that you are a fairy of the woods, what woods?

"All the trees and shrubbery and groundcovers in short all of the naturally and unnaturally occurring plants growth of the region."

I see, do you know me?

"Yes of course, we love the work you are doing in writing and talking to people about how plants are conscious. We are trying to help you as much as we can. We help with extra growth of the plants on your property and extra-long flowering of your plants and we give you a just a little more rain than the surrounding farms."

Ooh how lovely, I am honoured! Yes, I do enjoy it and appreciate all your help. What are your main roles in the region?

"I like to oversee the regrowth of the natural plants in the region and I also oversee the good growth of all introduced species. If they are doing poorly, I invite other plants angels that are specific to that species to come and meld their energy and expertise to that particular plant."

So you can import specialized fairies?

"Yes, something along those lines."

What else are you in charge of?

"I am in charge of all the waterways and creeks and rivers; I also oversee the health of introduced dams and underground waterways. Also the hills, soil, climate and temperature, rain and rocks and minerals and all the wild and introduced animals in the area."

Wow, that is a lot of responsibility! I am not taking you away from your work?

"No you are not disturbing me at all, we were meant to meet and to learn from each other. I can be in more than one place at a time, bi-locating I think they call it."

So you knew I would ask to speak to you?

"Yes, it was planned, I also encouraged you to ask, remember those little promptings when you were meditating."

Yes.

"That was me gently giving you the idea of how to contact me, with the permission of your higher self of course."

Do you spend much time in my gardens?

THE YEAR OF TALKING TO PLANTS: THE PLANTS AND FAIRIES TALK IN THEIR OWN WORDS

"Yes, quite a lot of time, firstly because it contains lots of plant varieties that need checking up on and also because it is so beautiful, we fairies love to spend time there amongst the flowers, trees, vegetables and fruit plants. And also because it is near a special rock formation that is my home base so to speak."

The rock in the neighbouring paddock?

"Yes, indeed you suspected that as much, this is an area where lots of fairies congregate and enter their other dimensional homes and also a meeting place and most importantly a place where good energies from the earth are distributed around the surrounding landscape and region. This is a very positive place and a sacred place for us."

How many kilometres does this place serve?

"Possibly 30 or 40 kilometres, it has quite a large, land refreshment area."

So where is the next one?

"At the next one is in a 40-kilometre radius all around in like a grid formation. Each and every area of the land, air and sea have a point such as this that refreshes the surrounding areas with beneficial energies. This occurs all around the world."

Do you visit my garden every day?

"Yes, and several times a day if not more."

So there is an over-fairy like you that visits everyone's garden in the whole world?

"Yes indeed."

That's great.

"Yes, isn't it?"

And farms and natural landscapes?

"Yes, that's the idea."

Are they all so friendly and happy to talk to people?

"Yes, over-fairies always are, they have greater powers than normal fairies and don't mind at all being disturbed, because you aren't stopping them going about their business."

How big are you, what do you look like?

"I am a little taller than a human, with a tall willowy form and a mauve and green colouring, long flowing blonde and brown hair, blue and green eyes and bronze coloured skin. I have two wings at the back for flight and small feet for walking."

How old are you?

"I am about six hundred years old and have been serving this region for all of them."

So human habitation, or at least European ancestry human habitation is just a recent thing, what do you think of it?

"It was always destined to be this way; why would I question it? The earth is a place of total free- will, whatever you do with the land is up to you. Our role is to make sure all the systems are operating correctly within those parameters. We can't stop humans degrading or polluting an area, we can only gently persuade them of other ways of being, if they are open to change."

"Don't get me wrong we love the new changes, we love all the human contact but we would like to help humans to be more in tune with the environment and consider before they destroy parts of it willy-nilly."

So do you think this region had more and better rainfall when it had its full complement of trees and forest?

"Yes, it was more predictable and regular, because of the amount of moisture in the atmosphere building up to cause regular rain."

Will it get better rain in the near future?

"Yes, indeed the whole of Australia is in line for a big shake-up rainfall wise. You will be getting more and more and on a more regular basis. Australia is about to become a magical tropical island of the South. It will no longer be able to rightly be called the 'wide brown land.'"

Oh that's amazing, will the changes happen peacefully and gradually?

"Yes, indeed all the new changes that are about to happen worldwide will be gradual and safe enough for people to walk away, if it becomes too wet or too dry. As human consciousness gets lighter and more loving, it will be making completely loving and safe changes to the environment only. There will be no dramatic, fast or cataclysmic changes all at once. These changes will be safe and gradual but the end results will be dramatic and beneficial to all."

Will all the animals of the earth be able to adapt to the changes?

"Yes, animals are often aware of changes long before humans are, they will be able to detect them and move on if a river becomes flooded or another dries out. There will be no significant animal extinctions."

How about plants and habitats?

"There will be dramatic changes and as you know plants do not have legs. Some will die and others, many others will take their place in other areas. There will

be a dramatic movement and changing places of plants, but this also will happen in a calm and natural a way as possible with minimal disruption to the existing ecosystems."

"The fairy realm are well aware of these changes ahead of time and will carry out what remedial changes need to be put into place to make all transitions in nature as smooth and harmonious as possible."

What about human cities, town and settlements, will there be much disruption there?

"There are some that have been built on inappropriate places and they will have to leave their abodes, some town folk will decide to move to better places, higher ground etc. Most major cities and towns in the world will be fine. This is why there has been a major influx of nature angels into nature's systems and also incarnating in human form. They are in a position to help the people, plants and animals make a smooth and happy transition as possible. Many people will not have to move or leave their homes at all and if they do the homes will be bigger and better and more desirable. God or All There Is does not want this to be a time of loss but one of great gain. It will be a joyful and jubilant time for all. You will see."

Do over-fairies like you, often have contact with humans?

"Only the ones that request it or are working closely with the landscape. In general, normal people will have more contact with the plant and animal and land fairies."

So you are also in charge of how much it rains in the region?

"Sometimes we have control over that if we wish, that is more from the sylphs of the rain and clouds. I will oversee the overall amounts and distribution, if it is too high or low, I will liaise with the air sylphs and adjust it accordingly."

The trees were saying that the world's rainfall and climate is about to undergo a change in the not-too-distant future?

"Yes, it is, it will be a safe transition for all so you needn't worry about it, but most of the climates of the world are going to change dramatically to a more comfortable warm and semi-tropical feel. Even mountain areas will get a little warmer but they will also be the cooler areas on the planet, and new mountains will suddenly appear, the ones that have always been there in the spiritual dimensions will suddenly take on 'real' dimensions, so the world and the landscape itself will take on different dimensions and shapes. This is a very exciting time in

the history of the world. You will all be safe so don't put any worry energy into the subject."

Asking for More Rain

Can humans put in a request with their local fairy-of-place for more rain if we need it?

"The fairies are always aware of what the human inhabitants of an area want and need. So this is always kept in mind when we manage the rain in the first place but yes, a special request for more will be considered and we always respond to gratefulness and appreciation of the rain that you do get. This always ensures a constant supply of all the rain you need."

How would a normal person ask for more rain?

"Just be grateful for the current rain you are getting, firstly put a request to the local fairies out loud or in your mind will be heard and the request will be considered with all the other requirements of a landscape."

What determines rain then, and the amounts an area gets?

"Precipitation usually follows the normal flow of air currents and convection from neighbouring forests, seas and landmasses and the cold and warm fronts and wind patterns. This is the scientific factors but the human psyche is starting to play a major part in these cycles too, this is why we are asking all humans to be grateful for what they are currently getting, a lack of gratefulness could culminate in a drying up of the rain, the exact opposite of what you desire so it is best to be grateful and thankful."

Am I able to talk to you on a regular basis if I call for you?

"Yes, that is the idea; I will come when you call for me."

So does the over-fairy of the region know all the human inhabitants in the region?

"Yes, they know them, they are also part of their over-care, overseeing all human activity in the landscape."

Can fairies read human minds?

"Yes of course, not every bit, but the open bits. All animals and humans and plants are capable of this and this will be a common thing in the future. This is not a negative thing but a great advantage to a civilization because things will

not be able to be hidden so easily. People will not be able to lie and get away with it and deceptions in society both big and small will no longer be able to happen. It is to every being's advantage to be able to read each other's mind; it is not an invasion of privacy so much as a new level of intimacy and honesty that will prevail the world over. You should rejoice. No more lies, deceit, or dishonesty, nothing hidden by business, government or individuals. Dictators will never again be able to hoodwink a country into atrocities; a politician will never be able to safely lie again. This is a great thing. With this great rise in public and personal honesty will come the habit of people self-regulating themselves where they will not need to be told what is right and wrong because all will know and know that it is in their best interest to follow it, people will live permanently in happiness and joy."

What is the difference between humans and fairies?

"Humans are purely physical (and spiritual) and fairies are both of this dimension and from others and are part angel."

I will talk to you a little later?

"Yes, I will enjoy that very much."

Acceptance, Gratitude, Love and Joy

Are you there Gentica?

"Yes, I have been waiting for you. I know you tend to write in the mornings."

It seems funny to talk to a being that I cannot see.

"Yes, but you know I am as real as the trees that you have been conversing with."

Yes.

"There will soon be time when we angels will be easier to see for the whole population. This will be a blessed time full of awe and wonder and great ideas and inspirations. The time has come to start recognizing and honouring nature in all its shapes and forms. From the plants in a pot on your doorstep to the grass that you mow on Saturday mornings to the very air that you breathe and the plants and animals that you all eat. Nature is all around you but many of you do not even know that it exists, it is just something to be ignored and rushed past, to be cut down and eradicated, a nuisance at best and an enemy at worst. This is all false construct of the human ego and the opposite of the real truth, that nature has

been created for you by God or All There Is for human's pleasure, enjoyment and sustenance. It is here to be appreciated, blessed and enjoyed. If you humans do not stat to enjoy and bless the very food you eat and the grass that you walk on, you will start to have problems with those very things."

Gratitude and joy are prayers of being

Do nature angels and plants pray?

"Yes, in a way, but our prayer consists simply of thankfulness, peace and joy. These are prayers and communications to God at its purest form. There is little need to do anything less. If you are thankful for what you have, all the people and circumstances in your life and the food you eat and the air you breathe and the rain that falls from the sky. That is all the prayers you will need. This positive attitude will naturally protect you from harm and will construct more good situations in your life that you can appreciate and love and enjoy. You see, to honour one's world and be thankful to God and the Universe is really so simple, it does not need to be complex, you do not need to enter a church to do it. You do not need to speak to a God intermediary such as a priest, you do not need to read a holy book. Just by appreciating, enjoying and loving and being thankful is all the prayers that God needs in this life or any other. Do you understand?"

Yes, I do, I was beginning to start to think this way myself.

"Yes, I know; you are in touch with life's core truths."

So appreciation is prayer, enjoyment is prayer and love is prayer?

"Yes, exactly so. Once you start complicating matters with holy books and 'holy' men you start dividing and removing yourself from the simplicity of the truth of life on earth. You start convoluting things, causing more pain, possible misunderstanding, confusion and worshipping other people and things and places without feeling love and appreciation and thankfulness but fear and obligation and self-righteousness. You humans have made worship and a religion out of what is simple and joyful and involves no-middle men or intermediaries. Just your relationship with God and nature and All There Is and God's love for you by

returning your love and appreciation with more rewards and blessings. In this way you can cause a never-ending loop of blessings and lovely things happening in your life. So you never need to think where next you will get your food, sustenance money and love from, because it will be a never-ending stream of love and blessings that will be given to you in a yearly, daily and hourly basis."

"You understand that when you are feeling at your most grateful and loving and blessed, that your life starts improving and becoming magically beautiful and then when you start feeling negative and grumpy that you cause a slowing down of God's goodness to you. By your own hand"

Yes, I have experienced this. I also have had to come to terms with loving, or at least accepting even those things that are negative and seem to be bad situations. It is only then that the blessings of those situations reveal themselves and healing and more blessings can occur.

"Yes, indeed you know it well."

So we can cause more rainfall if we are grateful for the rain we get and even for the dryness?

"Yes, you have got it, see the blessings even when it is dry and then you will cause it to rain more. It cannot rain all the time nor can it be dry all the time. Everything seeks to reach a balance in life."

So in the same way one could appreciate it when one doesn't have much money as a way of increasing one's money?

"Yes, exactly so, your next amount of money is just around the corner, your next fall of rain is just around the corner. It only takes a piece of gratefulness and contentment to bring it closer and then directly to you."

So the fastest way of filling any empty cupboard is to bless its emptiness?

"Yes, and to remember the times when it was full and to bless those times. A sense of contentment will bring blessings to you no matter who you are or where you are or what you are doing. It is thus the secret of prosperity is to remember that you are never without even if it seems you are without. For example, you might have no money in your wallet, see this as temporary lull in the goodness and wealth that God brings us all on a daily basis. Know that the flow will be restored to you when you start appreciating and enjoying and loving. If you do this continuously there will never be a lull or an empty wallet in the first place.

Do you understand?"

Yes, we are to not take reality too literally and realize that everything can be shifted in a positive way if we start loving what is.

"Exactly, the human ego has a habit of taking reality too seriously and makes up too many 'fairy stories' about it such as 'I am not good enough', 'I am broke' etc. which are not exactly true but the human ego makes them true when it starts believing them. The trick is to not pay attention to the ego when it starts panicking about an empty wallet or when something seems to go wrong. Even things that seem to go wrong, may be the right things in the fullness of time. Sit in gratitude even when your life course takes an unexpected turn and you will learn the lesson of steering true on the river of your life-course."

"Humans need to learn the lesson of acceptance when things seem to go awry, know that is only temporary, your flow of good is assured with acceptance, gratefulness, love and joy."

"The trick is not to differentiate between good and bad. This causes a divide that doesn't really exist. There is only what is and acceptance of what is, this causes seeming bad situations to vanish quicker than sitting in discontent. Discontent just causes more things that will give more situations for you to feel discontent about if that is your wish. God or All There Is, loves to grant you all your wishes."

Thank you, it has been an enlightening talk.

"My pleasure."

What Can Humans Do to Help the Fairy Realm?

Dear Gentica, we have music serenading us in the background.

"Good, I like music as do all fairies."

So I can call you a fairy?

"Certainly"

Can I ask you general fairy questions?

"Yes, no problems."

Do fairies play music?

"Yes, they do all the time; music is a very joyful expression of life."

Yes, is it performed live or recorded?

"Yes, always live. Live music is more therapeutic for both the listener and the player. But recorded music is good too, a second-best option."

THE YEAR OF TALKING TO PLANTS: THE PLANTS AND FAIRIES TALK IN THEIR OWN WORDS

What is the difference between humans and fairies?

"Yes, there are a few differences. Fairies are part physical and part residing in the spiritual dimension. They can come and go as they please. They also have keener psychic and spiritual awareness than the general human being. Fairies are part related to the plant realm so they are part human and part plant. This may seem impossible to your logical way of thinking but in God's Universe anything is possible. Nature angels are perfectly adapted to best help and keep nature's systems ticking along perfectly. Fairies also have reincarnation and age and give birth like humans and also spiritual advancement. They also have proud physical lives and relationships and they take pride in their work and joy in their lives. Fairies can think for themselves and also have egos like humans. They may form opinions about you of their choosing. They also are operating on earth which is a planet of free will. So they have a fair free range in the decisions they make and thoughts that they have. However, the nature of fairies is that they are bound to carry out their allotted task in the allotted time or else things on earth and nature's systems would cease to work in complimentary ways. Fairies have a job to do and they incarnate knowing that, so they carry on with their job no matter what. That is the role of the nature angels. Fairies are nature magicians and can manifest all sorts of things in order to properly carry out their tasks and to have as much fun as they can while doing it. So they have many spiritual tools available to them in order to carry out the miracles of nature."

What can humans do to best help the fairy realm in general?

"Yes, there are many things that can be done and the first thing I would suggest is for them to listen to their children, it is the children that are infused with the knowledge of what best to do in every avenue of life. This is one instance when the population in general must not defer to their elders but the young children coming through now. They know what to do."

"Other things that can be done are to limit the use of personal chemicals by way of deodorants, sprays shampoos etc. that are not organic, because they do not break down in natures systems correctly and are bad for human systems too. Household chemicals should also be organic and to limit the use of artificial synthetic containers and packaging made from plastic. This breaks down into harmful chemicals into the environment and causes mutation in the genes of humans and animals alike. Glass, metal, paper and cardboard are suitable packing materials that also should be successfully recycled. Petrochemical fuels

are also most harmful to the environment and should be phased out post haste. Humans could put pressure on car companies and demand green modes of transport to be made."

"Only organic chemicals should be used in the garden and cooperation with your plants and nature angels is preferable to sprays of any kind. Organic fertilizers should only be used."

"Every human can go outside right now and start talking to the plants outside. Many people will immediately get images in their mind and conversations in their minds. Have faith, these are to be believed, you all really can talk to the plants and even to the rocks and animals too. It is time to quieten your lives and listen to the subtle thoughts in your own minds, in this way you will also be better able to listen to your own inner guidance too."

"Believe that we fairies are as real as the thumb on your hand, we are your and the planets little helpers and we are here to serve humanity and nature's systems. We mean no harm; we seek always to be in peace and harmony and to do our jobs well."

"It would also be a good idea to start clearing up your diets, limiting the amount of sugar, salt, and white flour, white rice and other white grains and processed foods that are eaten. These can cause poisonous accumulations in human's systems and hinder them hearing their own guidance."

"More time spent outdoors in nature is advisable for all humans. Humans need the sun, moon, stars, clouds, sky, winds, air, trees, plants and fairies more than they think. Humans were built to spend most of their time out-of-doors not cooped up in artificial dwellings. If work commitments keep you indoors at least open the windows to allow natural air circulation. Everyone benefits from spending a lot more time out-of-doors, humans would get considerably less illness and would as a collective consciousness become lighter in their outlooks and more positive, joyful and happy. Lunch and dinner times spent out of doors would also lighten one's outlook dramatically and counter the effects of stress in the workplace."

"Human jobs and commitments to career are not as earth-shattering as they might imagine, more time spent in pleasuresome activities, would also lighten the collective consciousness of humanity. Joyfulness is catching; once more people start seeking out their own joy, many others will follow causing a resurgence of happiness and bliss for all."

THE YEAR OF TALKING TO PLANTS: THE PLANTS AND FAIRIES TALK IN THEIR OWN WORDS

"If humans could as collective and family units spend more time growing their own local food for sustenance in the family garden. Every family will have a gardener in it now, someone who delights in growing things and working with the soil. These people should be put in charge of growing food for the collective family unit, with the help of all those who feel drawn to gardening. In this way a considerable amount of pollution will be reduced by people not needing so much food being transported from one end of the country and world to the other. Family and local groups could band together to make communal gardens of people who love gardening and feel drawn to the land. This frees up those who do not like gardening to do other things, like cooking, or making art, music, writing, teaching, healing etc."

"Home-grown and own-grown food knows you and will grow to your own specifications, body type and climate giving you many more blessings than the current 'farmed produce', from animals that are mistreated at worst and not given the love and care that they need in order to produce healthful food. Your plants also need to be loved; otherwise they will not grow well or be good nutrition either. Food eaten should also be mainly fresh content say 95 percent in that is should be eaten within three or four days of harvest to keep in a maximum number of vitamins and life-force. Other food like oil and grains and dried and preserved produce can be eaten but not as the bulk of the diet, just as tasty accompaniments. Just by following these few food ideas human diseases will be reducing by 95 percent."

"Know that your garden knows you and loves to grow well for you, weeds and all. Respect the weeds too because they also have valuable roles in the cycle of life. Slowing down in your lives and spending time in more quiet contemplation in nature and reading and learning inspirational things is also much needed now. Don't always turn on the television, spend time listening to your own thoughts and feelings. Take time to do meditation, yoga, tai chi or other quiet disciplines in order to quiet you mind and release tensions from your body. A relaxed mind and body always draws more good things into your life, you are better able to follow your highest life-course when you allow some quiet time in your life. Physical exercise by way of sport or other exercises is vitally important for a healthy mind and body, preferably time spent in outdoor pursuits. Just a quite daily walk around your garden or neighbourhood is very refreshing for all people."

"Know that nature and the nature angels are friendly and always loving. We are here to help the planet and to keep things in balance. We and your own

angels rejoice every time you make a positive decision to improve your life and relationships with other people."

"Above all follow you heart and your joy for they lead each and every person to the things that will fulfil them the most."

'With love and blessing to you all.'

A garden without fairies is like a life without God.

Chapter 12
Getting Closer To Nature

Sitting in a garden with flowers is like being given a big hug, that leaves a smile on your face and a warm glow in your heart.

Gentica what is the best way for people to get closer to nature in their everyday lives?

"Yes, contact with nature should ideally be a daily thing. Go outside and eat you breakfast in the morning, your afternoon lunchbreak or your dinner in the evening."

"Plant shady trees in your garden where you can relax and eat under, read or otherwise spend time. Put seats in secluded and shady spots in your garden, touch your plants and love them. Send love to your plants, pets and rocks in your area, they will feel it and respond accordingly. Love the weather no matter what it brings, rain, storms, dryness, heat, cold are all good in their own way, even if it is to make you appreciate the mild comfortable days."

"Eat more fresh-picked fruit vegetables, nuts and organic eggs and meat. Eat only that which has been raised integrity and kindness and thankfulness. Eat only fresh (picked within three days) local produce. Drink more water, bless your water and food before you eat it. Thank your plants for giving you shade and shelter, colour, flowers and fruit, the plants will respond in kind."

"Touch the ground, a tree and plants daily to feel connected to the earth and more confident and full of good health and vitality."

"*Tread lightly upon the earth, clean up litter, use only organic chemicals, recycle, reduce and reduce your consumption or products that are essential to your existence.*"

"*Listen daily to the birds, listen to the sounds of crickets, dogs, cicadas and the wind. These are all healing sounds listening and appreciating birds is one of the great pleasures. Be sure to listen and enjoy a little birdsong each day.*"

"*Use your body, exercise in the open air wherever possible, Exercise done out-of-doors increases endorphins and life-saving beneficial chemicals that greatly extends lifespans.*"

"*Love your pets, treat them kindly, pat and care for them and talk to them daily. They really do hear you and know what is going on in your life, they love you unconditionally as does the rest of nature.*"

"*The sound of running water is also beneficial try to include this as much as you can in your life by going to rivers, the sea, lakes. Have ponds, waterfalls, birdbaths and sprinklers in your own gardens to increase the beneficial effects of feeling and listening to the sound of water in your garden.*"

"*Fire is a neglected way of experiencing nature's wonders. A campfire or barbecue are wonderful ways of adding the fire element into you lives and hearts, balancing whatever needs rebalancing in your lives.*"

"*Flowers are nature's holy gifts. Many exist for pure decoration alone where the plants regenerate themselves by other means. Flowers are God's gift to man, woman and child. See the way children gravitate towards flowers, they know how important and heavenly flowers are for the human spirit. Take time to literally smell touch and appreciate the flowers in your gardens or park to feel the blessings increase in your life.*"

"*Watch the clouds in the sky up above. What messages do they have for you today? Spend time outside at night looking at the stars and moon; they have many stories to tell you. Spend the time during the day for the sun to touch and bless your skin and being. There is so much love for you just waiting to be given to you, are you willing to receive it?*"

Thank you Gentica, that was lovely. Another question do fairies get sick?

"*Mostly not but sometimes when they spend too much time in close proximity to humans where they might pick up on some of the human's thought forms.*"

THE YEAR OF TALKING TO PLANTS: THE PLANTS AND FAIRIES TALK IN THEIR OWN WORDS

"Fairies have more positive mind-sets and are more in touch with their God-selves than humans currently are. They see themselves as perfectly pure and healthy and happy and that is the reality, they create for themselves."

Do fairies ever need a break, time off or holiday?

"Yes, everyone needs a break from the same routine from time to time the fairies like to vary their tasks and swap roles occasionally. They make time for regular social get-togethers and parties. They can also go on holiday if they see fit."

Do fairies have shops or businesses?

"No fairies are master-manifesters, artisans and craftsmen. What they don't have they can craft out of natural materials or manifest out of the blue. They are experts at working with energy and know how to create things where none existed previously. If they have a need, each angel can manifest what he needs on his own with no need for middle-men or buying places. When he doesn't need the item anymore, he simply imagines it out of existence."

Fabulous! Why don't we see evidence of fairy houses or possessions? Or even evidence of fairies being in our lives?

"Fairies are from another dimension than yours, they work in your dimension but they spend their time in theirs, that is essentially in your garden, but in another dimensional place of that space. As you don't see the fairies, you don't see their tools or houses either, it is as it should be for now. There will soon come a time when this will all change and more and more people will become sensitive to seeing fairies and nature angels. This will encourage more and more people to be open to the realm of spirit. It is called quantum awakening to other dimensions of time and space, other realities and possibilities."

Do fairies ever have accidents and can they get caught up in natural disasters like bushfires?

"Yes, they can have accidents although it is rare, they are nimble and careful. Even if they get injured, they are capable of healing themselves instantly. They tend not to get caught up in natural disasters like bushfires because they know about it ahead of time and make sure they are in another dimension at the time to avoid the tempest."

What happens to the tree fairies whose tree is lost or whose habitat is destroyed?

"Once a whole tree is lost, one attached to a tree like a faun perishes too and goes on to reincarnate after a while. One who is a free operating independent

fairy will be able to rebuild his own habitat from scratch. This is part of fairies' roles in the environment to recover and renew what has been destroyed or dies of natural causes. Straight after the fire they will get to work and will not stop till the re-building, re-planting and renewing has been done. An environment such as Australia has been built to cope with fire and even flood and the plants have remarkable powers of renewal."

Yes, it does. Does fire have an important role in the landscape of Australia, or can we avoid having major bushfires?

"Major out-of-control bushfires will be a thing of the past in a few years where you humans will be able to control the elements more with forgotten skills and the help of the fairies and angels. A rain cloud could be summoned for instance and you will be able to make it rain at will wherever it is needed. Fire does have its place in a hot climate landscape, where there is a lack of the other elements then fire takes over a helps cleanse and clear a region. It is a cleansing renewing element. Every now and then the earth needs to cleanse herself, but this too she would like to do with your cooperation so you help her stay clear and clean and assist the process. Fire or water are needed to clear and particular area. There are other ways that are long forgotten that could clear a place instead of the elements like the act of group singing and dancing, these help to rebalance the elements making way for renewal and a clear environment."

Do fairies ever use our possessions?

"Some who live in close proximity to humans may have a play with them, but otherwise it would only be out of curiosity or playfulness rather than need. There is always 'evidence' of fairies being in your garden if you look. Who opens and closes the flowers in your garden each day? Who fertilizes and sows more plants? Who causes the wind, rain and fire? Who lives in the earth? Who plants mushrooms for your delight? Who creates that fresh and loving atmosphere whenever you walk out-of-doors? Of course it is the fairies!"

Play

Are fairies playful like the mythical fairies in stories?

"Yes, they got that part right. Fairies can be mischievous, curious and playful, but mostly they are loving and dutiful to Mother Earth and her inhabitants. They are fully in touch with their inner child and loving it. This is really an authentic way of living and being and much more nurturing to the soul. It is a natural way of living for humans too but many are frightened to be like it for fear of ridicule. Nevertheless, those that let their inner child out and to have free reign in their lives are all the richer for it."

"Not only does it increase longevity but also one's intelligence and positive results in one's life. One is at one's most powerful when one plays; it is God's natural state for us. Every day humans should play at least once or twice in their favourite areas, say a sport, an art or a craft. Play on a daily basis wards off disease, quickens one's mind and heightens intelligence. It makes you magnetic to good experiences in your life. People will not be able to help themselves but to help you, give you things, open doors for you, the earth smiles upon people who know how to and regularly participate in play. It is one of the reasons why God made you in order for you to be able to play."

"Play should not be merely relegated to those that are young in age. Playfulness is a highly creative time and a time when you are open to the imagination from your guidance. 'Play is a serious business; the business of a life lived well and in full appreciation."

So there are no trolls under the bridge?

"No, no trolls there might be some fairies protecting and maintaining the river under the bridge but they generally get on with their own business and don't have the time or inclination to go around bothering any people in the area."

If the plant earth is a planet of complete free-will, is this applicable to the fairies and the plants too?

"Yes indeed, all fairies have a choice of what they want to do, they can check out any time they like but generally the job as a fairy is one of constant service and this gives them great joy so why would they want to change this? They love the earth and the plants and animals and rocks very much, the love to do whatever they can to make life better for everyone and everything including you humans, their incarnations here on earth is one of service with joy."

Can Fruit Talk?

Gentica, can the fruit and vegetables we have harvested for eating communicate with us?

"Yes. Surprised? Even fruit and vegetables that have been picked days or weeks ago or the rotting fruit or the fruit stone or seed, you can speak to the lot and get reliable answers from them. Surprised?"

Yes, indeed! Although if I talked to a peach before I ate it I might feel sad for the peach, like I ate it alive. So I might not talk to a piece of fruit or vegetable I am about to eat!

"That's understandable."

Gentica, what is your aura colour?

"Dark sparking pink, yes, it is me you are seeing when you see pink sparks of light."

That is very pretty. If I saw the whole image of you, are you pretty bright colours?

'Yes, pink and blues and gold and yellow.'

Are all nature angels colourful in colour?

"No some are quite dull and camouflaged to be the exact same colour of rocks or the plants that they inhabit. It depends on the individual angels and what their purpose is and where they live."

Gum trees, Do the fairies/plants mind if we pull out weeds in our gardens just to maintain beauty or physical order?

"No neither we nor the fairies mind that you decide to pull out weeds from anywhere. Even trees that are planted in the wrong place. We understand that there is a myriad of reasons as to why a human might want a plant to be removed. In nature we do not need noble reasons for plant removal, even if it is a frivolous reason. So long as it is not a complete destruction of a plants habitat like a whole field of forest or a whole forest for cheap profit. Ultimately it is you humans who will pay the price for habitat and microclimate loss. We can only advise you if you ask us but beyond that it is your choice."

"In regards to weeding your garden, it is all alright. We understand you want it neat and tidy. We understand you do it with love and no disrespect to nature or indeed the weeds, we know you use the weeds for mulch to care for your chosen plants in the garden that is totally unconditionally fine as far as we are concerned."

Unconditionally fine, a fine way to be! Are country fields surrounded by native trees and shrub thickets or hedgerows healthier than ones which don't have 'protection' on all sides?

"Yes, plant protection is always a valuable asset to a field farm or garden, this is also a harbour for native birds and wildlife and fairies which bless the land that they live on and increased the fertility of the surrounding area. A tree lined paddock is always more productive than one that is open to the elements."

Follow Your Love

It's very nice to sit out in the garden in the late evening gazing upon birds and dragonflies and butterflies going about their evening tasks in the serene stillness of the evening air. I often do my evening meditation out in the fresh air and some yoga moves on my lawn. I like to take my shoes off and walk barefoot on the grass for a very relaxing way of connecting with the earth, relaxing and recharging. A quiet walk on the cool evening grass is a serene way to see the day out.

Gentica what is the reason that we feel so good when doing these calming activities outside?

"Yes, all vigorous activities should be done outside to increase the number of endorphins that are released in the body. The cool night air and vigorous fairy presence in the mornings and evenings makes this a very healing and calming and enjoyable time for humans to spend outside. The fairies will often lend a hand if there is any healing work that needs to be done on a human who is outside. They clear anything or psychic debris that accumulates in a person's aura from spending a day doing various activities in various locales. This is all naturally cleared and balanced by the nature angels, all you need to do is to spend some time outside to reap these rewards."

"Peace giving activities like yoga and meditation are twice as powerful out of doors because of the help from the nature angels in helping you stay calm and clearing anything that is out of balance."

"Walking barefoot on the grass or touching the grass with your hands helps release any psychic debris that you may have collected. This is an excellent way of clearing yourself after a hard day out in the world."

"Time spent breathing in fresh unpolluted air and feeling the healing energy of the plants is a very calming thing to do whenever you have time to do it. Just sitting outside and doing nothing is also very calming, letting the sounds and colours and scents of nature lull your senses into a feeling of peace and contentment."

What secrets could the fairies tell us in order to live a happy and enjoyable life?

"There are two things; to live in the present moment only and by following love. Concentrate fully on what is at hand and the task and things you are doing at the time; this will imbue them with your natural joy and enthusiasm which will also rub off onto you and your life. A life spent being fully present is a full and enjoyable one because you weren't daydreaming all the way through it, you are living in the moment fully paying attention and drinking in the joy that is life, that is being."

"The other thing is to work with love, follow what you love, spend time with people that you love. Do every task with love and it will turn out beautifully and you will create your own miracles. Love is the creative force of the universe it is your highest and best creative tool. To do things with love is to live in constant joy, this joy then rubs off on all who have contact with you and your creations. Create with love and you can't go wrong. Even a job or a chore that is tedious like doing the dishes or ironing or washing the car can be elevated by accepting you have to do it sometimes and finding the best way to do it and taking care to do the best job you can. To fully concentrate on doing the dishes when you are doing the dishes. See the colours and designs, enjoy stacking and wiping them. Be present with the process and you will find joy even with mundane tasks. Even with tasks you don't like, you can find one aspect of the task that is fun and concentrate on that. This elevates your fun in the whole task at hand. In this way even sweeping the streets can become an engrossing and pride-filled task that is a much sort after thing to do."

Gentica, did you have a hand in that delicious thunderstorm yesterday?

"You overestimate my powers, but yes I did put in a little word with the clouds knowing that you were having a hard time trying to keep everything watered in the heat."

Well, thank you, that is much appreciated! So if a person cares for the environment do the local over-fairies bless the local gardeners with such favours?

"They certainly do. Some give more rain, some give less, some persuade the pests to move away from the area and others help the plants bloom a little longer and stronger. We do all we can for sensitive and kind people and gardeners. Whether they notice it as a favour to them is another thing, but you only need to look around your garden to see many blessings and little miracles afoot every day."

So we could be thankful for it by simply enjoying them even if we are unsure of the source of such wonders?

"Yes indeed, that is our best reward to have your pleasure and delight as a result of something we have done. We love that so much; you wouldn't even realize it."

Do you have any favourite flowers Gentica?

"Yes, I think the flowers on the Bursaria and gum trees are very cute and elegant and sweetly fragrant. From the other European imports, I like are the bearded iris flowers and the liliums with their large fragrant and elegant flowers."

Could we humans contact the fairies or the clouds directly and ask if we want more rain?

"You could indeed, and if it is in their power, they will grant you wishes when it is convenient for them."

What do the fairies think of the synthetic fabrics that we humans often wear?

"We do not like them much; they interfere with the body's natural electrical currents and aura and sometimes block your guidance. It is far better to search a bit more and find equivalent fabrics made out of cotton, wool, silk and linen and hemp etc. There are many other plant products that would lend themselves to fabric construction that have gone unnoticed."

Such as?

"Reeds and flax, gumtree and wattle bark, many other tree barks and fibrous leaves that can be pulverized and turned into a pliable and breathable fabric."

With crystals, rocks and dirt does the soul or elemental inside stay intact when a rock is broken into little pieces, how does this work?

"Yes, rocks are capable of division as in the case of cells so that each has its own elemental in charge of it no matter how small it gets. In the case of the soil it will speak to you as a whole mass rather than each of the tiny particle such as sand."

SARAH RAJKOTWALA

Chapter 13
Gentica Asks Me Some Questions

A change of routine can be as sweet as a holiday.

Well it seems the tables have turned and Gentica wants to interview me. I asked her what question she would like me to ask and ventured that she would like to ask me some questions for the book. So here they are.

"How does it feel to talk to plants?"

Well it felt uncomfortable at first and a little bit strained to remember to do it when I went outside. However, now I automatically go to ask them something if I need to without having to remind myself to do so. I have also had to ramp-up my trust in my own psychic and telepathic messages and to trust that the messages I am receiving are correct and genuine. I think this is because many of the answers have turned out to be true and have worked, thus I have taken on-board the other information to be reliable too. There has been much verifiable and checkable information coming through also, as well as unverifiable new spiritual information, but I know this to be reliable information. Like a conversation one has with a friend. One has to use one's discernment as a natural tool of being a human being, however. This goes for with psychic/telepathic things also.

You can tell deep down when someone tells you the truth. It feels natural and obvious. Why wouldn't we be able to talk to the plants and animals? The question is why has it taken us so long to realize it?

"How does it feel to talk to the fairies?"

Actually quite delightful, I can't help but put a smile on my face when talking about the fairies. They are so cute and I rather like the idea of little beings flying around taking care of all the little details in my garden and looking after our pets and wild animals. Just lovely and the fact that we can actually talk to them, fabulous. It is a delightful concept that fairies are real and helpful and it is even more exciting to be able to converse with them.

Talking to them feels fun and exciting and is a great addition to my life. I feel that this is just the beginning of a great adventure of discovering life forms that live parallel to ours taking care of the spiritual side of nature. With the fairies and indeed the angels. I feel that we have only just touched the edges of what we can do with this new and burgeoning conscious relationship with these entities. The sky is not the limit, there are unlimited possibilities with this new partnership between humans and the spiritual realms. The possibilities are wonderful with these delightful and inspirational beings.

"How has this changed your life (both talking to the plants and the fairies)?"

I think that we can now be friends and help nature and vice versa in ways that we never dreamed possible before. I now feel that I am not alone in my garden. We are never really alone in life; we have boundless limitless help from our loving Universe. I have lots and lots of little helpers who keep my garden running as well.

I feel some of my plant reference books will become almost redundant now that I can go straight to the source and obtain information it straight from the horse's mouth so-to-speak. Why deal with middlemen who only give you limited bits of information? Go straight to the plants who can give you reams of information on how they grow, what you can do with them etc.? The ramifications of what we can do with plants are a lot bigger than I first expected, there are whole encyclopedias of information I could get from just one plant.

It is no longer just my garden but a haven; a living area for hundreds of other little spiritual beings who know and care for my garden. I am not alone; all my movements are known by these little beings. I have probably been getting help from the fairies for years and didn't even realize it. I have probably been treading on and pulling out their work for years!

It is nice to know that nature's systems are all intact and we just need just need to stand back and let them repopulate the earth with forests and plants that are badly needed by our planet which needs more green cover to moderate its climates and provide good health and wellbeing for all.

THE YEAR OF TALKING TO PLANTS: THE PLANTS AND FAIRIES TALK IN THEIR OWN WORDS

It has made me more respectful of what is going on in my garden. I always had a respectful reverence towards nature but I am even more aware of not squelching something that has been put in place by the fairies for a reason or killing things needlessly that are conscious (plants). I am more mindful of my movements and if in doubt I can check with the plants. I still garden and pull-out weeds as per normal but I can also stand back and see what nature has in store for me and just knowing that reason and design has gone behind it, I find a rather comforting thought. Natures regenerative power is quite impressive. It can build life out of death, without us lifting a finger. If we only sit back a little and see what nature has in store for us, we could halve the amount of work that we do in the garden and enjoy more leisure-time.

Chapter 14
Questions and Answers

A question holds the answer in disguise.

It has been a glorious afternoon complete with grumbly thundery skies and delicious rain pummeling the parched summer ground in a determined deluge. Gentica, what can we do to show we have fully appreciated the rain and to ensure further supply?

"Just to feel appreciation, joy and gladness is enough, this alone ensures your supply of more. Things aren't as complicated as humans make them out to be."

I have a few questions of a similar nature lined up for you today Gentica.

Can you tell me about the significance of the following natural phenomena to humans?

Sunrise.

"Sunrise is the sacred time of day because our holy sun comes over the horizon to bless and spread love all over the land. If you get up early enough be sure to catch the colour of the sunrise in the morning, they help to awaken the chakras and to awaken the body's own natural timing systems, circadian rhythms. If one does not spend some time out in the sunrise, out in the open air, one can have problems sleeping and awaking and digestion problems to name a few things. A colourful sunrise is very healing a, consider yourself fortunate to experience these special sunrises."

Sunset.

"Sunset is the opposite of sunrise but equally important, it gives out colours and rhythms that slow down and synchronizes the bodies systems in order to have a good night's sleep and proper amount of quality dreaming time. If one does not go out in the open air at sunset time one can have problems, trying to get to sleep and waking up during the night. Just three days a week spent out in the open air looking or spending time in a sunset is enough to set you systems to their correct levels."

Sunlight.

"Sunlight is the warming food of love that the sun reflects back to us from ourselves, all the love one puts out is given to the sun to spread the love around the Universe. It is important for each human being to go outside every day and spend at least half an hour outside when the sun is out. The sun eases aches and pains and lightens one's moods and gets rid of grief and sadness and angry tendencies. Time spent out in the sun makes everything better."

Moonlight.

"The moon reflects our moods back to us, whatever gets us emotionally moody is reflected back to us in the different phases of the moon. The moon thrives on emotions and can regulate one's emotions better when spending at least three times a week outside at night to soak up the healing rays from the moon. The moon regulates all our bodies systems and helps get everything timed at its natural best, the digestive reproductive, circulatory, excretory systems etc. Time spent out in the moon enhances natural timing and helps with the Divine timing of everything in your life."

Phases of the Moon.

"Moon phases come and go; most people miss them completely and never really use them for the reason that they were intended at all. Time spent in the outdoors under any moon phase is beneficial and healing and re-calibrates your systems to be in tandem with natures systems, making you a healthier, more confident and powerful person."

"Each moon phase has its own qualities and power. But the following phases in particular are good for any work that human's might want to do in improving their daily reality via energy work, positive intention and imaginings."

Full Moon.

"Full moons are much maligned in history and nothing to be frightened of. However, the moon reflects that back what you have hidden away so others and you do not see it, let alone love or acknowledge it. The moon does us the service of bringing to the surface the hidden parts and fears that we have for us to acknowledge, love and release that which no longer serves us."

New Moon.

"New moon magic is powerful indeed. One can bring new projects closer to reality and fast-track things with the help of the new moon. Affirmations and positive statements said on the day and night of the new moon are fast-tracked into reality. It is a time to start new projects and ventures in order for them to have the greatest impact and best luck and velocity. It is all about celestial timing, time your projects with the cosmos and you can't go wrong."

Day Before a Full Moon.

"A charging time, a time to charge crystals and stones for personal use and to clear crystal and objects of others energy footprint on objects and even you can be

cleared under the day before full moon. Anything that you want to be rid of, say statements of release for any bad habits on this day and they will leave you quick smart. Time any releases for this day and night."

First Half-Moon

"The first half-moon is very powerful indeed it is the best for manifesting what you want in your life, that which you want to build up and keep in your life, affirmations and imaginings and energy work done on the half-moon day and night often come to pass."

Second Half-Moon

"The second half-moon in an important day to do energy work, affirmation, and imaginings on this day and night to bring to completion part and in-completed projects, such as a business deal that is halfway through, court-case or artwork or gardening project. The half-moon powers projects into these unfinished projects and finishes off the unfinished bits satisfactorily and wonderfully for all concerned, a very powerful day."

The Magic of Music

"Music is a sacred and beautiful thing. It is very healing both to hear and to make music or even to sing to yourself. Singing heals and brings into alignment what the body and mind needs to put into order. Music can also create things and clear things and move things. Music is the Universes gift to you all and you can use it for pleasure, healing, fun and purpose."

The Energy of Dance

"Dancing also is an excellent way for realignment of our emotions and feeling the joy of living. Dancing can be purely for its own enjoyment or for creating things, and harmonics in the environment to pull things back into alignment in the cosmic way of creating healing and harmony. Singing and dancing brings great blessings and release and protection into your lives."

The Healing Power of Joy

"Joy is a state of constant being, and feeling and totally living in the moment where you are fully experiencing life as you live it. That is all joy is, total absorption in your hobbies or projects or whatever that you find the most diverting, the most harmonious with your spirit. Joy is aligning you with your spirit, this is the perfect way to exist on the earth to be in harmony with all that is. Even a day spent in a little joy brings so many blessings to your life and rights and wrongs or mis-creations that you will wonder why you have been so blessed. Joy is essential to your soul; it is never selfish to spend time doing something you find joy in. This is your responsibility to others, yourself and the planet. Joy felt by one human radiates out into the Universe and comes back to you in magical burst of wonderfulness. That is what joy is."

"Joy is a love accelerator. It accelerates the love that sits within your soul and blesses you, your life, your loved ones and your region. Joy has the power to travel across the Universe doing good deeds as it goes. Joy accelerates spiritual enlightenment which cannot be obtained in sadness but in joy. Joy is the building block of the Universe. Joy makes everything better and alright; joy is God and the Universes gift to all. Spend some time in joy today."

The Blessings of Love

"Love is the very essence of creation it is God's tool of creation; it is the basis and truth of whole universe and multiverses. Love is love. Love is you, other people, the planets, and God. Love is in everything and can bring alignment to everything.

Love is the ultimate power, there is no way it can be misused or misguided, love brings healing and alignment and balance to everything. Love brings in light and acknowledgment and wisdom. Love is the tool for the wise. There is no one who doesn't deserve your love, there is no situation that doesn't deserve your love. There is nothing on this earth that doesn't deserve your love. All is healed in love's golden light. Love has its own intelligence and can get into situations and create miracles where every other approach has failed. Love is the first, last and only tool you should use in order to change a situation that isn't to your liking. Love is all."

The Consciousness of Water

"Water is a conducting element. It is conscious and intelligent and loving. It is able to change its structure when the intention to change it is there. Therefore, people can bless, love and otherwise imbue the water with healing powers in order to heal a body that drinks it. You can speak to water, water is capable of carrying on a conversation with you, whether it be a cup of water or a lake or a sea. It is all conscious alive and loving and able to give advice to those that require it."

The Calming Effect of Fire

"Fire is the bright and cleansing element that many people do not get enough of in your mechanized society. It is important to come into contact with fire weekly to make sure none of the elements are out of balance in your life. This is quite simple to do, just by lighting a candle you are contacting the element of fire and warming up your life and passions. Fire can be consciously directed like water and prayers or intention directed at an open flame have a powerful way of coming to pass. Use fire with love and intention and you can't go wrong. "

"Fire is warm, cleansing, renewing and refreshing. You will feel this way when you regularly but safely let fire into your life."

The Enlightenment of Air

"Air is the power of the sylphs flying in the air such as with wind and storms. Air seems gentle but it can lend strength and ideas and enlightenment into your life. Air is strong. Time simply spent outside in the fresh air and particularly on a windy day can feel revitalizing and refreshing."

"Air carries new ideas and new modes of thinking along with it, it can wipe the slate clean and bring new modes of operation into your lives. Spend some time out in the open air today."

The Stillness and Majesty of the Earth

"The groundedness that is everyone's right is the power of the earth. The earth keeps your feet on the ground when your thoughts are in higher dimensions. It is important to keep close contact with the earth and this keep your focus on the here and now and not on flights of fancy. The correct balance of all the elements in your life can rejuvenate a person and help them heal and move into bright new directions and to evolve and learn at your correct way and pace."

"Just touching the earth with your bare hands and feet can give you earth contact as can touching rocks, plants and crystals. Make a point of doing these things daily and you will be a well-balanced individual with a well-balanced life."

Manifestation

If we humans want to manifest something what is the best way of going about it?

"Manifestation is bringing into existence that which is not in physical formation yet. Sometimes these things exist in the ether world in another dimension just waiting to be manifested by a keen individual sometimes they are one's own designs that are put for safe keeping into the ether for future production when the exact universal timing is right."

"If one wants something one should think about it in detail in joy. The joy is the magnet that will draw it to you, the imagination is the artist creative tool and

the detail is designing it to your complete specifications. It is also to be imagined in the now, the present as if you already have the object you desire in joy. The joy is the real mover and shaker. If you start to do this manifestation work with ambiguity, sadness fear, anger, worry or lacking in confidence you will blow the whole thing out of the water so-to-speak. Positive emotions are what is needed and an absolute assurance that it is going to happen in faith. Design in your imagination with joy and you will receive with joy."

Oh lovely, thank you!

Working out in the Sunshine

On a completely different subject. What are the benefits of working outside in the sunshine?

"The sun lives on love and emits love, the benefits of being out in the sun are manifold but to keep it brief the sun gives you vitamins and love and nurturing. A life lived out of the sun would make you feel unloved and sad and quite vitamin depleted, the sun helps to absorb other vitamins that you get from your food. The sun gives you courage and happiness, and peace and contentment. These are qualities you get when you spend some time out in the sun every day."

What do fairies think of the human's 'climate change' and 'global warming' concepts?

"The fairies are amused at these concepts. Well it was the fairies' idea in the first place! They needed something to slow down the people's rush to pollute the earth! This is not going to actually happen, the earth has a way of regulating itself and will always have climates that are conducive to human, animal and plant habitation. There are no problems there. However, you will be going through a five to ten-year cycle of great world and climate change and extremes, until it gets back to a better kind of normal again, this is a temporary phase only and people are not to worry that it is a bad omen or portent of things to come. It is simple a readjustment, a realigning of the poles and equators to what they will be in the future, this is a time of great change and great enlightenment. The changes are all for the good and are very positive indeed. Don't worry about if there is flooding here or fires there or extreme temperatures, all will be revealed in a very short time. Have faith, live in love and appreciation of this great earth that we all live on, she loves and cares

for us all very much and won't let anything bad happen to us. Simply be with the changes and all will be well, if you remain inflexible and still you will have a more troublesome time of it. Just roll with it and intend to enjoy your life despite what is going on and you will."

What do the fairies think of humans spending a lot of their lives chasing money?

"We also think that is very comical, but we didn't invent that! We find it a little sad that humans think money is the only way you obtain your riches. Do not most of life's riches come from nature itself? A roof over your head is made from nature's materials, food and water, the weather, plants and animals that you eat and keep for company and enjoyment. The water that you use to play your water-sports on, the snow that and mountains that you ski on, the sea that you have your leisure yachts on, the hill that affords you million-dollar views. The beautiful holiday destinations on the Greek islands. It all consists of nature really. What comes from nature can be obtained for nature directly, you do not need money in order to obtain these things. Nature can give you what you need and does so on a daily basis. You just need to look around and appreciate what you have already and more will be forthcoming, both gifts from nature and the more earthly gifts of time for leisure and contemplation, good friends and of course money. Appreciate what you have in the way of money and more will be drawn to you like a magnet."

"In this way you can obtain money without needing to ceaselessly chase it or work you fingers to the bone. You can have your cake and eat it too. The trick is to love and appreciate the cake and more cake will come rapidly, in the most miraculous ways. Remember it is also good to give up the situation and surrender it to God and the angels and the situation will be even more rapidly give you what you desire."

Chapter 15
Time

Everything is relative, even time

Gentica with our concentration on time and measurement of time, how it is affecting and binding us to time?

"Time as you know it is a human construct, as you know we already have seasonal, equinox and day and night times to guide us. However, the measurement of years, days on calendars and the use of timetables and the prolific use of clocks, deadlines and starting and finishing times reinforces that belief that time exists, which it does not."

"Each time you look at a clock it reinforces to the human's mind that times exists. So it is a mild form of brain-washing, if you like. If time exists then you can run out of time, hence the need for ageing and eventual death. But what if instead a child grew to an adult and aged no more? This is entirely possible in a world without time."

"The time and space restrictions of this time traps you in, stops all possible belief and the possible exploration into different dimensions and different ways of being in the same place at two or more times. Which is highly advantageous from a point when time does not exist."

Soul Time

How does one stop being restricted into the belief of time?

"One stops measuring it as though it were a thing that existed. That which you don't give attention to contracts. So if enough people did it all at once (ignored time) and just lived their lives in soul-time they would suddenly be released from all the false and restrictive gradual aging, decline, illness and death that time belief constructs. If you believe you have time, and it is a destination then it has a beginning and an end. If you don't believe in it, it is endless. Life is endless."

"Without time, one is as free as a bird to explore life and to live and love and create in fun and in glory. Soul time is just following one's instincts and urges to do what one does throughout the day, without looking at the clock. In this way it is possible to expand and contract time, to fit more things into a day or to make a journey or day seem to run faster. Time is bendable, flexible and malleable. It is possible for a soul to be able to meld time according to the souls needs, not the other way around. Time can be like your best friend or your worst enemy; it just depends on whether you follow the world of human time or soul time."

"Soul time is relaxing, it is always right, its timing is always right, things always be completed on time. The disbelief in time gives you more time, ironic, isn't it?"

"We fairies do not exist in time at all. We think it is funny and somewhat controlled, that you humans run around doing things and then stopping doing things according to what the time is. It's like the clock and the calendar rule your lives."

OK so how does this affect our lives with say how to watch a television show at the right time for instance? How would you know if there is no time measurement?

"It is not the measurement of time that is the major problem but your belief that it exists."

"So one can still look at the TV book to see what you want to watch, make a note of when it starts. You do not keep looking at the clock to check it. Is it time, is it time yet? Constant clock-watching makes time. Leaving the timing up to the Universe deconstructs this false belief. You can still use a clock and calendar but not to rule your lives according to it."

So would it be good to live our lives as free as a bird and completely forgetting what month it is?

"Yes, that is good; you will always know what the time of year is because the seasons tell you. Measuring the time by the earth's rhythms, seasons and time of day (morning, afternoon) is the best way to live and measure things by. Like how you say 'new seasons peaches', instead of 'February peaches', this is correct. Summer strawberries, autumn apples, autumn harvest time."

So how about me marking all the jobs I have to do on the calendar?

"That's fine for your own record, you aren't marking time so much as saying this job here, that job there, making sure they are all covered."

"But what we are talking about is to live your lives in a freer more rambling, instinctive way rather than being restricted by time."

"We know you have had days with this experience where you saw them as ideal days. Where you seemed to fit in so much. A little art, a little reading for fun, reading for learning, writing, playing, eating, watching a movie, gardening you seemed to fit so much in and that is because you lived it by 'soul time'. You followed what felt good to do at the time, you followed what would fill you with the most joy and delight (in your words) and this is the best way to find soul time. Souls flow best when they are doing things they love to do and enjoy, when they want to do it. In this way and fully living in the present moment every job like doing the washing are intensely fulfilling as is entirely living in the moment and concentrating on just the washing."

It is true there have been several such days just recently where I did a little bit of many activities and followed what I thought would give me joy. In this way I also did work and housework but even these tasks were fun. I didn't overtax myself with any one job just a little of everything and a lot of leisure and fun time and by the end of the day I was amazed how much I had done and how it was indeed a 'perfect day'.

Gentica if people could see fairies would we all see all of them all at once or only what we concentrated on?

"All of them, once your sight and mind familiarize themselves with these images, the whole world of nature angels is opened up before you. Once your spiritual sight opens, all is revealed in its minute glory."

Do you think seeing fairies would help humanity respect nature more and stop polluting and destroying it?

"*Yes, certainly but it is not immediately necessarily, just to know of our existence is enough to start the ball rolling and to help people be more caring and sensitive to the environment as a whole.*"

So then fairies would want more people to be able to see them?

"*Without doubt, but they are patient too and will wait until people are ready to see, but like we have discussed there are more advantages for everyone to see the fairies and angelic realms, well it's all advantageous.*"

What is that urge that I felt when I've been inside too long?

"*It is your higher-self prompting you to go outside to get some fresh air and freshen up all your physical and mental systems.*"

The Energy of Trees

It is a very calming thing to have lots of trees around. Why do trees feel so calming?

"*Because their roots go far into the earth, providing stability, strength and endurance. As they are the tallest plants, so they have all the qualities of other plants only magnified many times over. There is a deep stillness and a timelessness with trees; beckoning you to join them in that timeless stillness and peace. Hugging a tree can give you some immediate calming benefits, it helps keep you grounded and feeling secure on Mother Earth.*"

Gentica when one meditates under a tree, is it enhanced by being next to it?

"*Yes, the trees lend their own qualities of deep peacefulness and centeredness to the senses as it does any person who sits under or near tree or hugs or talks to them.*"

"*Also the particular energies of the tree enhance one's being when you sit or meditate by them. Different trees have different qualities so if you sat under a different tree with each meditation, you would take on subtly some of the positive qualities of that tree.*"

"*Like under that ash trees you were just meditating under you would take on some of the qualities of strength and protection, you would feel a little stronger and protected when you spend time with ash trees. You would also feel more of a sense of safety in everything you do. This arises from the protective qualities of the ash tree. So this would enhance those feeling that you already have in that line and*" *strengthen them or lend that quality to you if you lack it. In this way too, spending time with trees is deeply healing. As you walk around, say after being around an ash tree you would feel more confident when dealing with the world because you feel more protected, these were the qualities that tree strengthened in you."*

"In this way nature can be a counsellor and a healer blending and enhancing your qualities with theirs with positive benefits. This is the role of the whole of nature. As the plants you are interviewing tell you the qualities that they specialize in, know that those can be used by every human or even an animal's advantage. By planting them in your garden and spending time tending, looking at or simply sitting near them and soaking up their positive qualities; this enhances your life on many levels."

"In this way one can consciously use the healing powers of plants to heal parts of you that need healing, rebalancing or resting. One can make a garden full of only peaceful plants if one has a restless personality."

A garden of only wise plants if one wants to gain wisdom or plants that specialize on love if you want to learn how to give and receive more love."

Do you see the practical applications of such knowledge?

Yes, I do, I am beginning to see how this all can benefit humans. On a personal level Just sitting under the ash tree I am feeling more protected, peaceful and still.

"Exactly the plants you are the closest to and the trees produce the most pronounced vibrations of energy."

So any plants or piece of nature can be brought into the house to lend these qualities to blend them into the household?

"Yes."

How about water and feathers?

"Water is extremely healing and balancing for the emotions. Anything that is out of balance can be encouraged to be into balance with waters presence."

"Feathers lend the qualities of the sylphs, freedom, quick thinking and awe and before you say it fire in the form of candles or lamps or a fireplace lends the qualities of warmth, passion and excitedness in a calm way, and love and dreaminess to a room. Each and every part of nature can be used for man's benefit both indoors and out."

Gentica, what are the qualities of rocks and crystals compared to those of trees and plants?

"They are very similar yet different. Crystals and rocks are very transportable and can be put in a pocket or jewellery for personal use. The rocks and crystals each have their own qualities that can be used for humanities benefit. Their prime benefit is that they are exaggerators of human energy and intention. They enlarge what is already there and with intention that can be directed in positive ways. They are crystalline matter and that is a very powerful generator of energy."

"Plants and trees on the other hand are living and breathing forms of energy and life and love they can be used in also powerful ways, they can lend their energies to any human who cares to spend time with them or their flower, wood, leaves or any part of a plant. They all have different uses and specialties, crystals, plants and rocks each have their own use for humans in their lives."

Another question. Does it just happen by itself? The healing energy of a plant or do you need to say sit under a tree with that intention?

"It happens all by itself, time spent in nature should be a relaxing and organic approach to healing, not striving and trying, rather letting and allowing. Just by letting the subtle energies of the plants wash over you and improve your moods, energy and physical wellbeing is enough. You do not need to intend anything with the plants; they will automatically work their magic on you. That is why nature is there, to automatically balance and maintain all of nature's systems and that includes the human systems."

So trees and plants live in the present moment, does this give them more power?

"Plants are all very powerful because they permanently live in a state of grace and bliss and they are living each moment as it comes."

More powerful than humans?

"More powerful than an unconscious human but not as powerful as a conscious one. But again it is not about power but of effectiveness in the tasks one has incarnated on earth to do. When you work with love and joy and fully living and experiencing the moment as it is you are adding a great many blessings and all of that love to the earth and to the Universe."

I am guessing my habit of concentrating on whether the weather is hot or cold, nice or not, this is part of me that still hadn't reached peace with the present moment and resisting what is and the beauty of what is, as it is.

"Exactly, that is why you will never hear plants complain about the weather, they just don't, they love whatever comes and deal with it as it comes and fully

experience life as it comes not filtered through a sad or unpleasant or even happy memory but just as it has happened for the first time, unblemished by expectation."

The Miracles of Flexibility and Manifestation

Roses, how would you describe your powers of rejuvenation?

"We would describe ourselves as survivors but also of surviving because we can bend and alter our responses depending on the situation. We don't stand rigid but we accommodate whatever is happening in the world and bend accordingly. In this way we don't snap from inflexibility or die because we don't like what we are experiencing. We go into another phase, shed what we don't need and survive because we remained flexible, come what may."

There they go again, the plants communicating so poetically and expansively from such a simple question. Who'd have thought your garden could think so broadly on such a wide range of subjects and have life-lessons to teach us as well? Thank you roses, that was beautiful!

This sort of thinking could help humans to take any severe weather patterns they might experience and flow with them rather than despising them just accept them and bend accordingly. Go with the flow, enjoy it even. This is a temporary thing in our world, our calm acceptance can precipitate positive change by calming down the weather patterns locally and then worldwide.

Gentica, can you tell me if there is a significance in seeing a single butterfly in the garden (I just saw the most gigantic orange monarch butterfly fluttering up and down the melaleucas which are in full creamy flower)?

"Yes, a single butterfly in your garden, particularly if it is near you or flies around you is significant. Butterflies are angelic messengers telling you that everything is going to be OK, you are on the right track and all is well. Like a big angelic hug!"

That's lovely, thank you!

How about dragonflies?

"The two are special messengers of a different kind. The dragonflies let you know that your loved ones in heaven are safe and cared for and happy. They also tell you that this is a time of change and of transformation and that all is well, another positive angelic report card."

Are there also other creatures that are favourites of the angels?

"Yes, beetles, ladybirds, bats, owl, robins, snakes and lizards. All animals play their part as messengers of different sorts and of emissaries of unconditional love, but some have close relations with the angels and fairies and can do good deeds."

Roses are so resilient, just when you think all is lost, they regroup themselves and start anew. Roses are truly a plant of hope.

Chapter 16
Mother Earth Giving Us Personal Gifts

We are a gift to Mother Earth and she is a gift to us

Gentica how important does the land need trees to cover it?

"It is quite crucial to the earths landmass regions, that two thirds of its surface area go back to tree cover. This can be in the form of street trees, gardens, community areas and public parks in cities and suburbs to replanting the trees back on farming land. The farmers could be paid to grow and maintain and have part of their land or all of it back covered in trees, shrubs, groundcovers, grasses wetlands or estuary systems whatever was naturally occurring originally before man's extensive clearing of the land."

"The earth and the number of humans that reside on the land today, need that many trees to sustain the environment, climate and air quality."

"The earth needs it to stop erosion and land degradation and humans need it to heal and balance their own systems as well as natures. Trees can be planted in highways and byways, road edges and hill tops. Houses can have plants built on top of them. It is important to counter the extensive use of paving and road surfaces and houses with the right balance of trees and plants to counteract the heating up of the atmosphere that too much non-planted areas can cause."

"The land, the waterways, the rivers and the seas need the correct number of trees and forests to clear and maintain their systems, water quality and sea life. More trees counteract human pollution and land-use and create a balance between nature and man's designs on the land. A balance must always be found and you would be surprised how creative man can be once he sets his mind to it."

Yes, indeed! I read somewhere that the earth knows each and every one of us, is this true?

"Yes, this is true the earth knows everyone who walks upon her, man, beast, bird or plant. The earth is conscious and supremely loving and wants only the best for all its human inhabitants. She knows each one of you by name and knows what you do for a living. She knows if you also care for the earth and its environments and to what extent but loves you all equally just the same."

"The earth sometimes rewards humans who do good works for the planet. Look out for unexpected windfalls of produce from the earth such as baskets of fruit or vegetables given to you unexpectedly, nature handcrafts or a bunch of flowers freshly picked from a beloved garden. A cutting or divided up bulb, a perennial from someone's garden to yours. These are all signs that the gifts not only came from the giver but from Mother Earth herself! A lush garden too is a significant sign that Mother Earth is looking after your plot of land."

I have many times been given such gifts. A basketful of bulbs or a bag of fruit or someone's divided up irises and I give such gifts often too.

"Precisely Mother Earth gives you through others and you give to others on Mother Earth's behalf. Look at the ones on the receiving end of such earth gifts. See how in some way they are doing their part in bringing joy of Mother Nature and a love of the earth to others and caring for her and her plants and animals as they would a child. Also look out for plants that produce fruit out of season, or flowers miraculously appearing on plants."

That is a most charming concept, thanks!

Concentrate on the Love

Gentica, I wanted to ask what happens to the tree fairies when a forest is pulled down and what happens to the river ones if a river dries up?

"Tree fairies fly away or get deployed elsewhere and the fauns attached to the trees perish along with the tree. It is not a sad time but a time of regeneration. The only sad thing is the loss of the forest for the remaining inhabitants of the earth who need each forest and natural area in order to live in balance. Some of the fairies remain in the region to re-sow what they can salvage of the vegetation if given a

chance. River fairies remain in place until the water returns. Sometimes this could be for many years."

What do they do in that time?

"They work towards making things better for that planet in the best ways they can until the water returns once again. Sometimes their dances and joyful manifestation activities actually bring the water again. Always remember to send love to the fairies of a river with no water; this will give them the strength to return the water once again and to continue on in love and joy."

"The love you send out to your beloved pets, plants or loved ones is never wasted. Love has a way of going off and beatifying the surrounding garden, atmosphere and world. Really beautiful and bountiful home gardens are always tended with a great deal of love or else great beauty could not be seen. Beauty always follows love."

'Beauty always follows love.' – Gentica, fairy of the woods

"It is the degree of love that you perceive in the beauty that makes it appear all the more beautiful. Something can appear beautiful without much love but it won't last for long and won't seem that beautiful to many people."

"There is love in everything or else it would not exist. Nothing on this earth or the Universe does not contain love. You can concentrate on that love that is inside everything to bring out it's more loving qualities. A person you are arguing with, if you concentrate on the love, they have inside of them, the argument will frizzle out and cease. If you concentrate on a bare ugly garden or the beauty within it, it will soon become beautiful and full and healthy. Concentrating and focusing on love makes you capable of many small and large miracles in your life and that of others."

Using the Elements to Improve our Lives

Gentica, I'm talking to you and the plants by writing it down, is this the best way that other people can get answers from plants or is talking directly to them just as good and accurate?

"Yes, good question, we find that for people either way is good and accurate, even for people who don't think they're psychic they probably are. Writing it down gives you a good record of what is said. Sometimes you don't have access to pen and paper like you have found with finding a leaking water pipe, it is just as accurate if not more so by asking in your mind or out loud and getting images in your mind via images of thoughts. I find the best way is to suspend your disbelief and assume that what you are getting is correct. I think this trust goes a long way to getting better and clearer information."

"When you talk to a plant look at them, ask a question and imagine that you are getting a response back. This 'imagined' response is often strikingly accurate. So your imagination is the conduit for information from the other realms, dimensions and species. Your imagination is where you receive all your personal guidance and it is also where you create your own reality, which we all do on a daily basis. Cleaning out your physical diet is also good for psychic work and for receiving your own guidance in the form of good ideas, images and feelings."

"Stilling your own mind with something like meditation, tai chi or yoga and spending more time out of doors in nature. Clearing out your mental diet of negative thoughts and feelings is also important. Negativity blocks guidance and attracts other negative thoughts to you. So stop watching the TV news and spend more time in nature and doing the things you love to stop the constant barrage of negativity that is pedalled as reality because in truth reality is what we make it to be. You all are part of the creator and are creators. You created the present reality from your past thoughts and feelings. Your future is created by your current thoughts and feelings and images and words. So be careful and disciplined in what you think and don't buy into so called negative world situations or your own if something negative has happened to you.'

"Imagine now a more positive future in the present tense with gratefulness as your emotional magnet and watch your future be created by you. That is after all how the world operates; it has just taken a long time for you to remember it."

"Synthetic chemicals in food and chemicals substances like chocolate are no-nos as far as receiving psychic information. They blur and dull the psychic senses."

Negativity is a silent prayer for less than you want.

Gentica can a bowl of flowers be made with say a variety of fragrance themes?

"Yes, you could say choose flowers with a theme of peace, love and harmony or a theme of strength, freedom and independence or beauty and clarity and appreciation. The choice and combinations are endless and people will soon be able to have fun combining such natural scents for their indoor decoration when they learn about this phenomenon."

God-Made Fragrances

What about chemically made perfumes and deodorizers?

"Well you know the answer to this; they are not of the natural world and hold no qualities except from the factory and test tubes where they were made. Their scents are artificial; the human response that they inspire is artificial and leaves no long-lasting beneficial effects. In fact, many are detrimental to the human olfactory senses. My advice and that of the other fairies, is to steer away from any chemically made perfumes, deodorizers, air-fresheners and the like and go for real fresh air. Walk outside; open the windows of your house. Bring a bunch of flowers, leaves, berries or freshly picked fruit inside and feel the effects of real God-made scents."

Can flowers say roses without a scent be as effective?

"Flowers with no or little scent are not as effective at carrying the ideas and feelings. That is the purpose of scent as a carrier for energy."

Synthetic Fibres

What about synthetic fibers that we wear? How do they compare with natural fibers like cotton, wool and silk?

"All the natural fibers bless and caress the body and add certain blessings. Synthetic fibers interfere with the natural electrics of the body system and do not add to one's life but detract by way of not letting the body breathe properly and causing excessive perspiration."

Does the same go for synthetic blankets, quilts and bedding?

"Doubly so, one spends a lot of time in bed and one is not fully conscious to be able to pull down an overly hot quilt. So this interrupts sleep and causes excessive perspiration and even bad dreams from being in a light and constantly woken sleep."

Charging Water with Thoughts

Gentica can water be changed either positively or negatively with our thoughts?

"Of course from river to seas, streams and ponds, and baths; a bowl or glass of water or a single drop. All can be altered with the human mind and imagination. One can think any properties onto it and it will be so."

Is it the same with wind, fire, earth or a rock?

"Intention can be directed at any of the elements for man's advantage and the advantage of others or the environment. All can be altered and improved just by the quality of your positive thoughts. This is an area of great potential for man."

Can we put positive thoughts into the watering can of water in order to feed love to the plants?

"Yes, indeed this is exactly what you can do, programme the water, infuse it with your love that will then go down to the little roots of the plants and be of more value to them than anything else."

Can we add positive thoughts or thoughts of things we specifically want to heal to our drinking water or bath water? Can we do it with the shower water too?

"Yes specific healing or even better add love to your drinking, bathwater and yes even the running shower water. This way you bathe yourself with love. What better way is there to start or end your day?"

"In a glass of drinking water or water in a vase you can also add love thought or peace, send it peace and for that day and the duration of the flowers in the vase both the flowers and the water will exude peace into your room, house and family."

Wowy kazowie, that's huge!

"You can also put love thoughts into your drinking water which is the best thought to beam everywhere because it has the highest frequency and can achieve the best and most miraculous results."

Oh this is very interesting. So the elements like water, fire, air, wind etc. are porous and are capable of soaking up our thoughts or turning them into reality here quickly?

"Yes, precisely think a thought, wish or intention as you light a candle or look into the fireplace, these thoughts are being transposed into reality with the help of the loving and very capable elements. These are meant to be your tools and your friends not your enemies and are there to enhance your lives and not detract from it. They are your loving gifts from God to use, to create a life you love. See you weren't born here without tools to use in order to make you lives richer, healthier and happier. You have, built into nature all manner of tools, guidance, medicines and foods for your every need and desire."

Chapter 17
Asking Permission To Prune

You don't need permission to love.

As a keen gardener it is with some trepidation and guilt that I now realize that plants are fully conscious and are cognizant of what we are doing to them. Ash tree, what do you have to say to people who make a living from plants and we who like to prune plants in our garden from time to time?

"Yes, we think it is funny that you should be so worried about our feelings. We say yippee there is someone who at least cares about us. If you make a living from pruning and tending plants, so what? We love that; more people should love nurseries and garden centres so that more plants are distributed about the population as a whole to help humans get into a permanent state of wellness."

"We don't hurt when people prune us but when people ignore us or harm or pollute the environment this is what upsets us. Someone pruning us in love or to give to someone who'll love us in turn is an act of holiness and supreme love. Calm your mind and consciousness about this situation, you are looking at it the wrong way around. Where we are tended in someone's gardens or workplace, it means on some level that they care, this is positive. So is it when people come into close contact with us via touching, pruning etc. It is all good, don't worry your head about this."

Alright, that's a relief thanks. Oh, one more question. Do we have to ask permission when we take pruning or cutting of fruit or cut flowers from a plant by way as a warning?

"Yes, we would like a bit of warning if you could remember to do it, it helps us prepare ourselves both physically and psychically."

How much notice do you need?

"Only a few seconds."

What about if we pick fruit, do we need to ask permission for that?

"Yes, we would like that too, not permission so much as forewarning of your intention, we tend to pick up on your thoughts anyway but it helps us in preparation."

OK, thanks I'll try to remember and be more thoughtful to the plants. I do thank them now for their fruit or produce. Could I say prepare say a whole rose or vegetable garden in advance that I'm coming around and talking cuttings or fruit from a whole garden to save asking each individual plant?

"Yes, that's the idea, just state your intention to the whole group or garden of plants either aloud or in your head and we will get your message."

Thanks I was thinking otherwise it would be too cumbersome asking every plant when you are pruning a whole orchard for instance. Do trees or plants form bonds with their people/owners?

"Yes, they do, each tree or plant in a person's garden or vicinity knows about them, their thoughts, feelings and lives. In this way the trees or plants are in sympathy with their people, they follow their lives and care about them when they are sick or angry or in any way out-of-sorts. Plants consider people, the people who garden amongst them, their people. Particularly people who give love and tender care to their plants and gardens, they have their loyalty and love for life. Even if they subsequently move house, they follow your lives and send love and care to you. It is a very positive thing to love your garden and your plants. You never know where it may lead you."

That's beautiful. Are children able to talk telepathically to plants and if so more or less so than adults?

"Children are able to talk telepathically with plants, even more so than adults, they have been less sullied by the world's ways and have a pure and fresh and unbiased perspective on what messages they get. It would be good to teach children from a young age to talk to their plants."

Gentica, if fairies are half physical creatures how come we haven't seen them?

"We are there; it is because you humans don't believe we are there so you don't even perceive of our existence. Most children readily see fairies and angels and the like and get howled down by their parents, the children sense their anger, discouragement, disbelief and even fear from their parents and learn to close off

their psychic instincts so that they fit into the acceptable 'norm'. However, what if the 'norm' wasn't really the best option for humans? What if it was the second best and even tenth best options? The very best options would be to believe in the existence of angels, fairies and your own guides and to actively work with them and to give them your love and belief."

Tall Tree Protective Energy

Gentica, why does it look and feel so good to have tall trees grown behind houses? When I see a photo or a painting it always looks better and more ideal when there are tall trees and shrubs at the back and the sides of a home.

"It is for the protective energy that trees give off. Trees ground a house and protect it particularly from winds and rain and pollution and also psychically a house is protected by the powerful presence of tall trees. Trees give an energy of calmness and stability; this infuses the area with this energy, particularly the residents of the nearby house."

Is it because of their size that makes them powerful?

"Yes, being the 'whales' of the flora world trees are the realm's most powerful representatives of peace, stability and love. Trees anchor the landscape in this energy and in a sense anchor a house that sits in this landscape. Trees like whales are emissaries for peace and eternal love and presence. An area that has less trees has a slightly more unstable feel to it, witness people in desert areas, they aren't always as calm as the ones in forested areas. This is in part has to do with a lack of trees to bring their calming presence to an area."

Why does a thick forest of trees behind a house feel so good in particular?

"The thickness indicates the thoroughness of the protective forces that the trees and plants can give a house and residents of the area."

Natives Versus Non-Natives

What do the gum trees think of the different and non-native varieties of trees, shrubs and plants that self- seed on the side of the roads?

"We celebrate any plant variety that can beat the odds, self-seed with the help of the fairies and thrive and survive with no care, the occasional agricultural spray, car exhaust fumes, and abject neglect."

Pioneer Plant Species

"The olives and other assorted fruit trees, roses, pines, ashes and other assorted introduced species to Australia and other areas have an inbuilt toughness for such exposed locations and have a knack of being easy to sow from seed. These plants are pioneer species and add an important and integral part to the ecology and badly denuded and deforested areas. Every plant that has self-sown along nature strip and the edges of roads trees and shrubs and need to be rewarded and loved and thanked for their resilience and toughness against all odds. This energy of toughness and resilience then moves out to the farms and farmers and neighbouring towns giving them the strength to survive tough and good times alike."

The absolute acceptance of the plants of other plant varieties has surprised me somewhat. Not that I expected them to be adversarial, but maybe a little cool towards other varieties, particularly non-native ones. This couldn't be further from the truth, and I am pleased to find in reality that they embrace all living things with their inclusive attitude. We humans could take a leaf out of their book, so to speak!

"Do not underestimate the power and purpose of wild plants whether they are native or not. If there were native plants and trees there that could have re-sown, they would have done so. The fairies aren't stupid; they have calculated the situation and carefully chosen the species that would do best in areas of denuded landscape. As you have found out the indigenous natives that were part of forest communities are very hard to replace and put back when their community of plants and fairies has long since gone.

It is the role of these pioneer species to fill the void left by the decimation of the natural balance of the environment, these pioneers may be the forerunners of a whole new species mix for that area. You can't turn the clock back once a forest has been gone for over a hundred years. You will have never be able to exactly duplicate what was three before because you'd need the right sort and number of insects, birds, grasses, sedges, groundcovers, possums, kangaroos, small marsupials, fairies and native peoples to exactly replicate how it was before, and these elements in that balance are long gone. It is up to nature and the humans to find another balance, what is going to grow there now with the natural rainfall and insect mix? Waterways may have dried up and been disturbed. Great tracts of land have been cleared for farming, rivers have been dammed and diverted.

Everything has been altered from its pristine wild origins. It is up to the current inhabitants to allow the wisdom of nature to take its course and choose what species it best sees fit for those neglected areas and let them thrive and survive because that is what they will do if left to exist in peace."

So this is the reason why I have had more bother trying to establish and re-grow the indigenous native species on my property?

"Indeed the conditions that they had when they were the dominant plant species are no longer there. A new set of circumstances has arrived, so try to adjust to it. Still try to grow the indigenous when you can but other natives that are stronger may be appropriate for your area where not a bush, shrub or tree was left standing in heavily farmed and cleared areas."

Chapter 18
She Feels Every Step

"She feels every step; she knows what you feel.
When you love she loves, when you laugh she
laughs, she is your Earth Mother and she loves you
so."

Gum trees do trees sleep?

"Yes, we do at night when you sleep we do; we gently exhale any cares back to the earth who transforms them into love for us. We awaken a few hours generally before humans do and go about our daily tasks of transpiring, cleaning and sending out vibes of love and wellbeing and groundedness."

Gentica do fairies sleep?

"We sleep only for a few hours in the early hours of the morning, needing only a few hours' sleep before we go about our daily tasks again."

Are the hills I live on conscious, as a separate entity like you?

"They are, each piece of God's creations can be divided into ever decreasing parts and particles, each individual part is conscious in its own right and can be communicated with. On the other hand, increasingly larger entities such as rocks and boulders, hillocks, hills and mountains and the earth itself is conscious and can be communicated with, each has its own intelligence."

Great so would communicating with a hill or mountain be different than communicating with the rocks that make it up?

"Yes and no, a hill or mountain is much wiser because of the combined wisdom of all its rocks and crystals within it so speaking to a mountain; you would get more profound insights."

Can anyone speak to a mountain the same way I am speaking to you?

"Indeed, everything is capable of clear and understandable and intelligent communication via mental telepathy, the Universal language."

Why haven't we discovered this before?

"This is because seemed too fantastic to modern scientific civilizations, there is no proof or logic of such things, but one day when the female energy of the planet is fully awakened people will see that a lot of logic is illogical and a lot of what is illogical or intuitive is in fact the more sensible approach to life."

Can each individual cloud be communicated with?

"Yes, just the same."

Does a plot of land that one lives on, can it be communicated with?

"Indeed that would be possible."

Does the land that each human lives on automatically know us?

"Yes, it knows, loves and assists you in every way it can. As part of the whole planet 'Gaia' it is incredibly powerful and tender and loving to each living entity on it and cares for each individual ant, plant, fairy and human as she would her own child, because you are all children of the earth. The love she has for you and for each individual human is so profound, deep and all-encompassing that it's hard to put into words."

Thank you, that's lovely.

So every living thing on this earth is conscious and intelligent and is capable of communication. That's amazing. One should never get bored with so many things to talk to, even if you've alone in the human sense.

Gentica, what is important about the energy of earth tremors or quakes?

"Earthquakes are a release of pent-up emotion that the earth has ingested from its human inhabitants. The more the build–up occurs, the more it has. The earth is much more sensitive than people realize and infinitely more intelligent. There is nothing that goes on the earth that she does not know about. She loves all her residents but she finds the humans the dearest to her heart because you are who the earth was built for, this is your playground your domain."

Thanks.

"She feels every footstep, every sneeze, every laugh. She participates in these activities and in human lives too. She sends you much love and adoration. She knows humanity is about to make a great leap and rejoices on your success at reaching this stage. She loves you all most dearly."

How about when we dig in the ground or mine it, does it hurt the earth?

"No it doesn't hurt as such but it does destabilize her systems when she is misused or mined inappropriately, with greedy intent and much suffering for the miners and poor wages. If the mining is done with advice from the nature angels and done with pure intent and love, then the effects are a lot different. Digging does not hurt the earth when it is to put in a plants or a pool. But if it is to dump rubbish or another negative act then this is not conducive to the good health of her systems."

If we touched the earth with love when we are gardening does she feel it?

"Yes, she does and she sends back your love in a great wave of love and adoration. When you appreciate the earth in this way many miracles are possible."

Gnomes, Devas and Leather Sandals

Gentica, I read somewhere that if Jesus were alive today he would be wearing plastic sandals because they cause less damage to the environment than leather ones, is this true? I have always preferred to wear leather shoes myself as they breathe. What do you have to say about this?

"Yes, you are quite correct, it is a misnomer to believe that just because a product needs lots of water to produce it is bad. It is also wrong to assume just because an animal is used somewhere in the process it is wrong. Animals were put on this earth for human use and companionship, as long as they are treated with honour, kindness and respect, and allowed to have as natural a life as possible out in nature there is no harm in killing an animal for its hide if the whole process in done with reverence and respect and thankfulness, this is proper. There is nowhere in the production of plastic and other synthetics where there is a proper and natural course of action. These things were never born, they never ever lived nor were they conscious. They are an inert soul-less manmade material that does damage to the ecosystem in each step of the production, transport, usage and disposal processes. Plastic is reluctant to break down and when it does it produces toxic chemicals

because that is what it is made out of in the first place. Jesus would undoubtedly have worn leather or other sort of natural fibre sandals or gone barefoot, as would all of your other religious leaders."

What about if everyone in the world wants to wear leather shoes?

"That would be fine, you are already producing enough beef, goat, sheep and pigs to process the shoes that you need by way of the meat production. It is just that most of the hides are thrown away or processed for compost."

Fairy Sub-Categories

Gentica in other books about fairies the authors mention all sorts of different names for different fairies. Is this correct do they have all these wondrous names and if so, why haven't I been told many by the plants and you?

"Yes, there is in existence all sorts of different titles for different nature angels and devas. We find this interesting too, not all of the names have come from us, they are more human inventions and we think they confuse the issue and causes a separation between different fairies which is not true nor useful in people's comprehension of us and for the first-time introduction to them, in particular."

Do you call different fairies different names?

"Sometimes but not often, we communicate with their own names and don't say 'Gnome come here', we would use their proper name, it is only polite after all."

"We prefer to be called fairies or nature angels and for people to also ask us and consider us as a whole rather than lots of little separated parts which is not how we tend to operate."

OK, what is a deva?

"A deva is a walking nature angel, more land-based rather than air-based, like the ones who have wings."

Are you a deva?

"Yes and no, I am a kind of a deva, but this is where distinctions are not helpful because many of us nature angels have slightly different builds and roles but are still doing the same job. We all work together in a Divine and natural tandem movement."

"It is like saying there are Chinese and Indians and Africans but really you are all people and all have variations but lead similar sorts of lives with similar sorts of aspirations."

Yes indeed. I'm sorry to seem to be one tracked minded but are there such a thing as gnomes, I do get your point but you mentioned a gnome and I was curious?

"Yes of course there are, they are a form of deva because they are land based and they often work with the earth or underground or with stones. They are kindly like all nature angels and do look a little like the mythical ones that people characterize as garden statues. Which by-the-way the gnomes really love. They think this is a form of thankyou and respect for all the hard world they do in keeping the earth's systems balanced."

They all seem to be male gnomes are there any female ones?

"Yes of course there are roughly fifty percent of each but the humans of older times had a higher opinion of the males of the species and do not think that women could work as well as men so overlooked them and wrote them out of their stories."

*W*hirlies Venting Energy

Gentica, a farmer was ploughing up his paddocks yesterday, creating a lot of topsoil to fly in to the air and surrounding area. Then a whirly seemed to emanate from that area and build up in a swirling momentum. It seemed to be in reaction to the vigorous ploughing of the dry ground, as though it was conscious.

"Yes, it was, the nature sylph that caused the whirly was venting his displeasure in such a rough use of the land, as you noticed there was a lot of flying-away of the precious top soil."

Okay would this have affected the sylph in any way?

"Yes, he is in charge of the wind currents and air of that particular region and doesn't like the air to be filled with such a precious resource in such a deliberate way."

So all whirlies and tornadoes are conscious?

"Yes, they are."

Are the whirlies always a venting of energy?

"Mostly, it is a venting of elemental emotions."

Do they, the wind currents and tornados and whirlies have sexes like male or female?

"Not necessarily, sometimes they do but mostly they have no gender at all."

So each elemental also likes to protect the other element's resources too?

"Yes of course we are all in it together we are all part of the same earth and universe."

I always had a sense of, even years ago that nothing we do in the garden goes unnoticed. I was then just talking about birds and the insects following and noticing your every move. However, I now know I also sensed the nature angels and their conscious attention to all my garden improvements. I wonder if they follow us around the garden watching our ever move with interest and even helping out where they can?

"Yes, this would be a correct assumption. They do follow humans around with great interest, they like to participate and help where they can. This is while a little later in the season, those very same plants say like petunias magically re-sow somewhere in a pot for you to play with and plant in the garden like you planted the others. This was the fairies following you around and noticing your interest in a particular area and trying to help and participate in your gardening experience. The earth is highly conscious as are all the elementals and fairies and they all like to help kindly humans and gardeners wherever they can, watch out for their helpful hand. If it looked like the fairies have helped you in your gardening pursuits, then they probably have."

Asking a Plant if it wants to Come Home with You

Should we be asking plants where they would like to go in the garden or is it best for us to choose the spot or both?

"Yes, it would also be polite to ask the tiny plants where in the garden they would like to be planted. Of course this has to be tempered with where you would like it to go. Like asking guests where they would like to sit at the table, sometimes

you might have particular reason to choose the seating for the guests. Either way is alright. It is your garden, you can choose all the positions for plants yourself, or if you want a little more success, then think where you want to put it and okay it with the plants, if they have any strong suggestions, they will let you know. You can also go about this by tuning into your feelings, feel where the best spot for this plants would be, chances are you will get it right this way too."

What about food, I read that your body knows what food is good for you, you just need to put it near your solar plexus (tummy) and if it feels drawn to you it is good for you and if it feels repelled by you it is not so good for you, is this correct?

"Quite correct, you could also ask the food itself if it is an alive food such as a freshly picked apple or sunflower seeds, or nuts. If it is a dead food, meat, bread, processed food then use the solar plexus method. You can even employ your feelings here too, what do you feel when you contemplate eating this product? If it feels good then is okay if it feels indifferent, or sad or bloated or a little anxious, then don't bother eating it."

The Benefits of Being Outside

I have been thinking that many people do not spend enough time out-of-doors in nature for its health benefits. Gentica, can you explain exactly what happens to humans when they spend some time outside whether it be sitting on a bench or walking or sport or anything?

"Yes, a rise in their feel-happy chemicals, the endorphins and melatonin happens after a short time sitting out in the sun and fresh air, say after 15 minutes. This gives rise to good feelings that last for the whole day. If one spends time out of doors in the evening this lasts all of the night, the time can be spent sitting or lying outside or doing activities like walking, gardening, yoga or tai chi or sport. The fairies immediately start working on clearing your aura from the minute you step a foot out of doors. Your body starts re-calibrating itself to nature's natural rhythms and the sunlight and wind and fresh air start cleaning your lungs of any toxins that you have taken in by spending a long time indoors."

"Out-of-doors is humans natural home, the human body is meant to spend most of its time out of doors, not indoors. It is not made to be shut up away

from sunlight, fresh air, the moonlight and the powerful healing effects of natural wonders such as sunrises and sunsets, rainbows and even the healing effects of feeling snow, rain and fog on your face and in your pores."

"Foods that are freshly picked from nature and eaten out of doors are naturally more nutritious and fill you full of the joyful life force of the plants that you plucked it from. You are feeling more naturally joyful by spending time out with the plants and the fairies. Nature is God's antidepressant and at least an hour spent out of doors in full sunlight (summer, winter or any time of year but not sitting under a big, covered verandah), will go a long way toward picking up one's mood and maintaining it to its own equilibrium."

"Ideas and concepts of a spiritual nature and all higher learning is better comprehended and assimilated when done out of doors. Inspiration, whether it be artistic, scientific or spiritual is more likely by 90 percent to happen out of doors. Nature is man's true inspiration and muse and helps unlock one's own intuition to gain Universal knowledge, wisdom and second sight."

"Put simply, one puts oneself at a disadvantage in every way, physically, mentally and spiritually when one closes oneself off from nature by spending the majority of one's time indoors."

"Children who spend more time playing outside are naturally, fitter, healthier, get less colds and suffer less bad moods and tantrums. This also includes teenagers who would benefit from even more time spent out-of-doors in order to make the transition from childhood and adulthood more smoothly, successfully and enjoyably. Sport activities, outdoors eating and resting areas, barbeques, and games can all be played out of doors. When eating out choose places that have outdoors eating area such as casual cafes so that maximum outdoors refreshment can be had. People who spend more time outside are less overweight and healthier in their heart from constantly exposing themselves to the healing power of nature. There is no coincidence that gardeners seem healthier than the general population and people who participate regularly in outdoor sport. They are getting multiple health benefits like talking a multivitamin for life, for the life-force which cannot be obtained indoors no matter how alluring and attractive they make it."

"Spend a minimum of one hour a day outside and notice the change in your mood and positivity and prepare yourself for more inspiration and insights, and above all enjoy yourself. Whatever you enjoy doing indoors you can do out-of-doors. Knitting, puzzles, board games, cooking, entertaining, watching TV and movies,

*even napping are all more beneficial when done outside in the loving arms of
mother nature and her dominions."*

Big and Small Victories

Gentica does the earth feel it when we plant a new tree or plants into it?

*"Yes, why would it not? The earth is highly sensitive and feels every footstep and
every sigh and every emotion felt on her, and she stores up these emotions. Every
now and then when the storage levels get too much for her, they vent out as volcanic
eruptions earth tremors etc."*

*"Likewise she loves and celebrates with you your big and small victories. Such
as a successful fruit crop, a job promotion or the birth of a baby. She knows when
she has more greenery planted into her by the humans and the fairies knowing
that humans are simply larger version of the fairies, without wings. She knows that
each new tree and plant planted upon her goes towards making the whole exist in
equilibrium and she sings in the gloriousness of how such a simple act by you can
mean so much to the whole. Small simple acts are not small; they are profoundly
effective in making the earth a better place to live. If you choose to make your
own veggie garden or choose to plant a tree or windbreak in your property or buy
recycled paper, this is never a simple or small act, this is all noticed and adds to the
great well of love, care and joy that is available for all to use every day."*

What do you mean we can all use the love and care?

*"By existing in a state of love, by feeling love, by caring for something, you then
tap into the joint energy and wave of love and caring that all humans have done
for eons, and all the love that is generated by non-incarnated beings like angels and
fairies etc."*

Ok thank you, that was beautiful. So my one small action of planting one
tree or shrub and the act of caring adds to the great well of caring all around the
planet and beyond?

"Exactly."

Clearing Trees to Build a House

What do you think gum trees about people clearing off natural scrubland in order to build their own house and garden?

"We love every combination of this. If people enjoy nature enough that they want to live out in it then well and good. If they want to build a house then great and if they want to start a garden of their own, excellent, we couldn't be happier. Earth, this planet is all about man and his relationship with himself played out in the backdrop of nature. If man wants to spend any time out in it in a self-contained garden, be it native or no-native, we don't mind. What is important is the fact that he ventures into nature and goes outside to enjoy it. I bet you are surprised by our response?"

Yes, a little.

"Understand that nature is all inclusive not exclusive. We do not want only our plant variety to the exclusion of all else. We (the trees) have benefitted immensely from you planting your garden around us and enjoy it and you spending time in it in love and joy. We follow the process and enjoy the process with you; the joy you send out into the universe is the important thing. How you do it is immaterial; it is the joy and the love that is important."

OK, I see.

"Don't get us wrong. Large tracts of forest and natural habitats should be protected for humanities future use. But small quantities of it used for domestic dwellings, gardens and a few sheds or a small farming concern are most welcome and indeed encouraged by the plants, nature angels and Mother Earth herself. It would not be harmonious to only have lots of forest and no dwellings if the people needed it. It would not be harmonious to not let people change the use of the land as they so require it. Giving proper respect to the environment and taking the suggestions of placement from the fairies and angels of place for optimum placement of houses, roads and other buildings. Until the time when everyone can converse with nature themselves, we are content that you look within and do what feels right, that is often the correct answer anyway."

So if one finds one's perfect block of land it's OK to knock down a few trees in order to create your dream home?

"Yes precisely, within reason. Obviously, areas of remnant native scrub that is almost extinct shouldn't be removed nor whole forests for a large farm, but a

reasonable clearance in order to grow an orchard or keep a few animals is highly acceptable if not desirable. We would love for everyone to have their own farm if they would like it or their own garden, that is nature's ideal scenario where the whole earth's human population has innate knowledge and daily contact with nature as much for humanities' as well as for nature's sake."

So nature needs humans?

"Certainly does a lock not need the key? Humans unlock the potential in nature and us in humans. It's a symbiotic relationship that is mutually beneficial and desirable."

Your words are delightfully enigmatic. What secrets does humanity unlock in nature?

"They wouldn't be secrets if I told you, would it?"

Well no, so these secrets will unfold as they should in the fullness of time?

"Yes precisely."

Plant Cuttings and Soul Memory

Gentica, I saw on TV last night that there was a plant that was grown from a cutting taken from a battlefield. My question is, do plants grown via cutting or offset carry the memories of the parent plant? If so, would it be good, energetically-speaking taking plants from former battlefields?

"Yes, they would have memories of such times like an ancestral memory but it has a completely different plant soul/fairy spirit so it would be starting from afresh so you don't really need to worry about any negative situations that the parent plants experienced as such."

So say with my old roses even though they are part of plants from centuries ago, they don't carry a historical memory of such time because each cutting is like a new incarnated plant?

"Yes, just so, a fresh cutting that takes root is a new life, a fresh division from a parent plant is a new life and a seed from a parent plant is a new life form."

Do plants have memories from their current life and do they have unique personalities?

"Yes, just as you, their soul part, the fairies carry memories of their particular incarnation and also others and yes they do have different personalities which is a culmination of all the experiences they have had in this life and others."

What about the part of the cutting that was a part of the parent plant when it was living and having those experiences?

"This memory is wiped when they turn into a separate plant with a separate root system so they can start life anew. Like people do when they have a different incarnation."

OK that's good news. Gentica do the fairies and the plants naturally clear areas such as war grounds and places where humans have left behind many negative thought forms?

"Yes of course this is part of what fairies are here for, working on places and areas that are heavy with negative human thought, but also it takes quite a long time to clear such things and many of these place are not places out in nature they are built-up cities without many plants to help do these jobs and the clearing can take much longer. Also if the humans choose to continue the negative ways of thinking, then this delays the good fairy activity and delays the eventual clearing of the place. We really do need the human's help with this and to realize that they

always have a choice, to remember they can choose thoughts of and acts of peace and love, even in war zones it is possible to think apart from the general population and to make a stand mentally and emotionally. Choosing peace is the most joyful choice one can choose and it helps other people think peaceful thoughts, even if you are just sitting in your house thinking kind, loving and peaceful thoughts."

"War grounds in fields and natural areas are often already cleared naturally, built-up plant-less cities can take hundreds of years. Planting plants trees and shrubs in cities and choosing to live in areas where everyone can live with gardens is another way to live with the fairies to enable them to help clear the atmosphere of the natural daily things that need to be cleared, without leading to any imbalances and build-up of human psychic garbage so to speak."

Gum trees how do you celebrate God?

"Hmm, good question. We celebrate simply by enjoying the life we have so generously been given and by living in joy in each and every moment. If we are not in joy, then we strive for it and it becomes so. There can be no greater celebration of thankfulness than by enjoying God's gift to you in every way that you can."

Thank you, that was lovely.

Chapter 19
Sacred Spaces

Sacred spaces, special places. It is all holy here, if you believe it to be so

Autumn is an exciting time in Southern Australia. With the cool and the rain come renewed planting potential and the start of my serious gardening again The ground is thick with seeds of future plants, the rain gives life to everything again. So many possibilities. I feel grateful for all the help the little folk give me!

Gentica, what role does one's love of the garden, play in the garden space?

"The garden and the plants the attending fairies simply thrive on the love that their human inhabitants have for the area. This is the icing on the cake, if you like and appreciate a garden, this turns the space from that of pure natural beauty to a sacred space. A space of love and purity and joy. This one little garden then has the power to affect the world and other people around it because of the peace and love and joy that emanates from it."

Wow, really? So when we love our garden, we create a sacred space for the planet?

"Yes, indeed that is how it is, this love and light then become available for all to use in the same way and to increase love and light in their lives. You can tell a loved garden as soon as you walk into it. It exudes something else other than all the parts of it, something extra, enchanting and magical. That is the feeling of a beloved sacred natural space. All the attendant fairies also pick up on this love and care and in turn are capable of more miracles and love themselves. That garden

then takes on a rainbow-coat of pride, producing more beauty and bountifulness and love."

Wow, that's great! I will have to pay more attention next time I visit people's gardens.

What about people's houses that they love?

"Yes, that is also the same. A beautiful feeling but not quite as magical as a living space, which is what a garden is."

How about people's gardens where they find it a chore to garden?

"Then the space will not seem as beautiful and some of the magic will not come out because it was hampered by negative thoughts and feelings of the inhabitants."

Alright. Is that a definition then of a sacred space?

"Yes, that is the definition of a sacred space or site, a natural area that has had loving feelings impregnated into it."

There's yet another reason to go out into your garden and to enjoy yourself!

Putting Love into the Equation

Gentica, can you tell me what the effects on say fruit and vegetables when they are planted with love?

"Yes, love put into the equation when it comes to anything but particularly to fruit and vegetable plants, produces what you would describe as magical effects for the end eaters and consumers of the products. They can produce miracle cures to long standing or chronic diseases and improve the health and vitality of an otherwise healthy individual beyond all expectations, giving them much improved constitutions. They will be more impervious to heat and cold and have more physical endurance and strength."

So all a gardener needs to do to produce this is think thoughts of love when they are planting the seeds?

"Yes, any thoughts of love. It can be love of the seed and of nature or of God or love of the family and people you will be growing them for or loving thoughts of oneself. All will work equally well."

So that is it, to produce those miracle results?

'Yes.'

No other little tips? Why have people not discovered this before?

"This is because you have walked around for many centuries with 'blinkers' on. It is not anyone's fault; it is simply time for humanity to move up to what is their birthright. The secret is that love is the highest power of them all. All who use it produce miraculous results without even trying or knowing how they are produced, suffice to say that love is the answer. Humans, as pieces of God can wield love with such powerful force that the whole Universe sits up and takes notice."

"Anything in nature (God's paradise for humans), when worked on with love produces wondrous and miraculous results. This could include working or making things like musical instruments out of wood, houses out of wood, dirt and stone. From working with rocks and crystals and the soil itself. To treating your animals, nature and the pets with love, rainclouds respond really well to love. Try it next time some crossover your house and you will notice that they will be inclined to rain on all those who love them. Musical instruments that are crafted from wood or dried vegetables are and made with love produce the sweetest music of them all and produce miraculous healings and feelings of love and contentment when in turn they are played with love."

Wow, like a love chain. Now the sun, what is really the sun's role in human's lives?

"The sun in a magnetic attractor for love. All love felt on earth is reflected and sent off to the sun who then magnifies and reflects back this love for all to use back on the earth."

How beautiful, thank you.

Is there any equation that does not include love?

Seeing Fairies

Gentica is it correct to say that to see fairies one first needs to believe they exist and then remove one's fear of seeing things psychically? Is this correct, and are there any other things that people need to do in order to see fairies?

"Yes, you are correct with the first two points and the only thing I would add is to look forward to the joy you will feel when being able to see them. Instead of it being a scary thing, it is exciting and fun to be able to talk to and see the nature angels. Not to mention highly beneficial to your understanding and usefulness in nature and gardening and working with nature and all its systems."

If one does see them, would one see larger beings going about their business as well as small fairies? Are they beings of light, lit up or would they look like insects real and fleshy?

"Yes, good question, I imagine it would be a combination of the two concepts. You would see a solid being which appears solid as well as lit up from within."

Alright so once you see them you will always see them?

"Yes, that is normally the way it goes. Once it becomes the societal norm to see such things then the children will not lose their psychic sight of such things and everyone will believe and understand the roles of the fairies in the nature realm."

Great that's something to look forward to.

Putting Back the Balance of Trees

Gentica, the hills around us are quite bare of trees. If they had more trees on them, would it attract more rainfall to the area?

"Trees produce moisture in the upper atmosphere resulting in eventual rain. Trees equal rain. All unused hills, valleys and gullies, roadsides and council lands should be filled with trees and shrubs and groundcovers to balance out the bare areas that agriculture has produced."

What percentage rainfall increase could we expect if more trees were introduced into the area?

"A twenty to fifty percent increase in your area, and larger or smaller amounts in other areas depending on their geography and morphology."

Trees, Wealth and Good Health

What other benefits could be expected with more trees planted in previously bare agricultural land?

"There are many and varied benefits from greater habitats for birds, mammals and marsupials. A gradual increase in the amount of topsoil available in an area where tiny particles for the upper atmosphere are trapped and fall to earth where there are stands of trees and help keep in the soil that otherwise would be lost on windy days. An increase in the wellbeing of an area for the plants animals and the human inhabitants. This is primarily because of the increase in the fairy activity and the increase in the clearing capacity of the land now it can breathe via its new trees.

More wealth for an area is a pleasant side-effect of more tree cover; trees always produce more wealth energetically not the other way around (i.e. pulling down trees). An increase in the bird life also increases the healing effect of birdsong which is vital for the human souls to feel good while living on this planet. An increase in the equilibrium of the insect population and the end of plagues of things like earwigs, locusts and aphids. Which are dissuaded when there are enough trees to supply enough birds to home so the birds keep the insect population in balance and in check. Why do you think God put all the trees there in the first place? It wasn't for decoration; it was for their function in maintaining the earth and the delicate ecosystems of the earth in order to properly and healthy maintain the human and animal populations on the planet."

"The rivers, streams, ponds and watercourses will also start working properly when there are enough trees to promote enough rain and this will keep the watercourses working at their optimal levels providing man and beast with many watering points. The air quality will go up and pollution levels will go down. The effects of wind and erosion on the land will be minimal as will the salt levels in the soil. A state or a region with its tree cover levels restored to higher levels can expect an increase in its wealth both spiritual and actual wealth to increase. Trees are a very good investment in Mother Nature and for your human society. The evaporation rate will also go down a little but this is enough to promote healthier growth in garden plants in surrounding gardens and parks."

There is no balance, if there are no trees.

Can Bulbs Talk?

"Yes, they can like seeds they emit conscious thought forms that humans and others can pick up on. You can ask them what sort of bulb they are and they may give you an image of their flower or the like."

If I picked up a fruit stone, could I ascertain whether it was a peach or nectarine by asking it?

"Certainly of course, nothing ventured, nothing gained. They are all capable of giving you information about themselves."

How does one ascertain from a fruit seed whether it will produce tasty fruit for you?

"If you liked eating the mother fruit then the seed will differ little from it. Also hold the seed to your heart, if you get a good feeling then it will be a tasty and good variety for you. If you feel nothing, then discard the seed and try another."

Chapter 20
Genetic Manipulation

Some issues are so not part of God's plan, the question almost needs not be asked

It's a delicious early winters day. The fog has crept up to the house, enveloping us in a soft blanket of loveliness. Fog always seems so cozy to me, like we are being given a big soft cloud hug.

Grafting

A few questions Gentica. Is grafting plants onto other plants a good practice? Can you elaborate on this subject?

"Yes, grafting is in a sense genetic manipulation. What God and Mother Nature have produced for us is already perfect and full of all the perfect qualities and nutrition for human beings, plants animals and all of nature's support systems. Once you start manipulating and adulterating what was already given to you in a pure and pristine state then it renders it adulterated and poisonous to both the environment and to humans. Grafted apricot trees, for example, put two different varieties of plant and blend their sap together. The grafted plant is always in a sense fighting the sap of the mother plant it was grafted onto and vice versa for the grafted rootstock. This energy of fighting and resistance then goes into the whole plant and flavours the plant and its fruit and nuts; they give off the energy of resistance and fighting off foreign bodies. This then leads to humans taking in

that energy when they eat the fruit and their bodies start fighting with themselves, leading to diseases such as autoimmune diseases where the bodies start fighting themselves. Also food allergies can result in eating this food."

"The best food to eat is that from food that has been grown from naturally occurring seed. Seed from an apricot for instance that has been grown from an apricot you just ate with appreciation. This stone then grows into a tree that is full of the energy of love and appreciation and grows as God and the earth intended for it to. Grafting has primarily come about by man's greediness in wanting to keep certain plant varieties to himself for profit without realizing that the seeds of fruit and grain are free for all to use and to grow from. Nature is free for all to use."

So what about my grafted fruit trees? Is there any value in them?

"Yes, eat what you are getting from them it is better than store-bought fruit at this stage. Eat it fresh from the trees, but long-term grow your own fruit trees from seed of fruit that you have liked the taste of. You have already started to do this. Long-term it is these that will produce the healthiest and tastiest fruits for human consumption. In this stage it is a matter of degrees. Do what you can, with whatever you have is the best option you have available to you at the time. When the options get better, choose them. Do you see?

Genetic Engineering

Yes, I do. What about plant selective breeding?

"Selective breeding i.e. choosing seed from a plant with certain characteristics and mating it with another with another set of characteristics is a fun pastime and thing to do and the fairies have no problems with this, they do this all the time themselves."

"Genetic engineering however and splicing certain genes onto others and genetically engineered foods are and aberration, are dangerous to both humans and the environment and can lead to humans turning into mutations themselves. Hold onto the bans in genetically engineered foods. Do not let politicians change the laws so that they do not need to label such foods. They are not to be consumed under any circumstances. A lot of packaged food in the US at the moment contains such items. Big companies are trying to make this spread the world over for no other reason apart from world domination of the food market and to make more money *and to hold the power over the human food-chain. It is for this reason that we fairies ask humans to start to grow their own unadulterated food from their own seed, freshly procured from fresh organic food."*

"Grow it for yourself. Grow your own food from what you have eaten and grow your own fruit as much as possible. Share with your friends the freshly picked fruit and produce that they too have grown with love and share the love and the natural goodness of fresh produce the way God intended it to be."

Self-Sufficiency

So the fairies like the idea of self-sufficiency?

"We love it; it is really a fairy-borne concept. To be in charge of the food you eat, to know where it came from, and giving it your love and attention is a blessing to both the grower and the end consumer. The environment also benefits from this and self-sufficient people also tend to not use chemicals and toxins on their own food. We love it."

Food and Water in Plastic

Does the water we drink need to breathe? If so, does this mean it is no good to transport water in plastic bottles for human consumption and what about plastic rainwater tanks?

"Ok a few questions here. Transporting your own water to drink that is obtained from as natural a source as possible is good for the time being. The best way is to bring water fresh from an unpolluted stream, river or spring or collected rainwater. The metal tanks are the best option at the moment. Steer clear of plastic because it is unstable and adds it chemicals to the water making it impure, no matter what the manufacturers say. Using plastic should be avoided. Carry water in a natural wooden or glass container when travelling or maybe a metal thermos flask. These are more stable natural materials that leaves the water in nearly the same state as it was put in. Let the water breathe, keep the lid off to allow it to aerate. Or have a hole in the lid. Water is alive and conscious and dies if the

air supply is cut off from it even for small periods. Dead water is not healthy for humans to drink; it leads to diseases."

What about food wrapped in plastic?

"When more of the human race start growing their own food on their own plots of land there will be less and less reason to buy food wrapped in plastic from supermarkets and this era of food bought in packages will come to an end. There will be a rise in people growing and eating fresh food and storing food by natural air-drying and preserving. There will be a rise in cooking your own food and treats and sharing with your friends and neighbours. The love and sharing the food that was lovingly grown from the earth with your own hands and bread that was baked with your hands, made and consumed with love. This will lead to greater levels of health in the human population, eventually leading to the natural elimination of all diseases and where the human bodies will not be harbors to disease and malaise. They will be operating as God intended them to with perfect health, happiness and joy."

That sounds wonderful. I always have had the urge to grow a large vegetable garden and to be as self-sufficient in food as possible.

Why do the fairies think we humans have got our agriculture out of balance with great big farms buoyed by mass food consumption eating up the last remaining wild habitats and rainforests? Also how can we do a better job at farming and feeding the world?

"The world can feed itself. Self-propelled prosperity and the enthusiasm for growing one's own clean and fresh food will eventually make the need for large farms null and void. In will come instead small boutique family run operations that grow specialized products for the small local markets. This will employ more farmers and make a living for anyone who wants to farm for a living and they will make a good one too using up less space. When more people take control of the lifecycle of their food they will not want to out-source most of their food growing. When people also realize that freshness and eating local produce is actually better for your health than eating imported produce from even the next town, they will settle into a cozier agrarian and nature-filled way of living closely with the environment and taking control of their own food needs in the main."

"Families growing their own food doesn't mean more toil, it can be an easy thing to do with the cooperation with the nature angels, angels, birds and animals

and the plants themselves then people can work in the garden and toil less and enjoy more."

Do the plants know when a human is sick or out-of-sorts or an animal is unwell?

"Yes of course and as soon as the person goes outside, we send them healing energy if not before. We plants love our human and animal companions so much that we do everything within our power to help them stay well and happy and at peace.

Nature is a very healing place to be. If you ever feel unwell or in a bad mood spend some time quietly sitting outside for say fifteen minutes at least and feel how much better, you feel at the end of it. Nature loves you all and gives you a huge nature's embrace every time you venture out into it, that is what we plants, rocks and the dirt was designed for."

Fairy Selection of Weeds

Gentica, I was wondering about the issue of weeds which I still find intriguing. Does it mean that all weeds are in a particular location not through random or natural selection but rather a deliberate fairy selection?

"Yes, you are quite right. The fairies are the real selectors in this instance. They choose the right plants for that particular spot on the ground and from the selection that is available to them in a particular area. If more varieties are available than the fairies might make a different set of choices but they always want to plant the hardiest plants varieties and the ones that are assured to grow well in that area."

Why don't they concentrate on growing the native plants to that area?

"They will, if given the chance and the native plant material, but if they do work them into the mix now their natural predators and balancers are often not available anymore. Some native plants need certain marsupials to eat and bury the seed for pollination for instance or a certain bird to eat the fruit and then the plant will grow from those droppings or a particular ant to bury the seed into the soil. A lot of the correct or same factors are needed in order to rejuvenate native habitat to what it was. If all the plants, all the groundcovers, weeds, seeds, possums, birds and insects, even the land has changed, then the sensitive habitat can't be turned back to exactly the way it was unless man gives a helping hand by returning some of

the species into the mix. However even then you can't turn back the clock, not every aspect is the same as before so things need to be adapted to the current conditions.'

'It is not a matter whether it is native or indigenous-native but bare hills can at least have transition varieties or plants that help to bring back the health of the land and then to gradually introduce the natives back once that tree and plant balance has been redressed. Even then everything has changed, the land use has changed for the land. Nature respects all the changes man makes if they are made with goodwill.'

'It is all good if man returns the greenery balance back to at least double what it is today even with the current farms and cities in place it will radically change things for the better no matter what plants are used. Naturally if there are sufficient and the right balance of native plants left say close to an empty field, just to close a field off and do nothing to it for a few years will be enough for the rest to restore the balance of native plants and once that is established for say ten years that little field will in turn supply the seed for the next field that can be enclosed. All the work does not have to be done by man, we can meet him halfway, if he allows the fairies with goodwill to re-tree areas that aren't being actively used by humans, like the tops of hills, wastelands, sides of roads, edges of farms of spare fields in farms. The rewards by returning parts or a portion of one's farmland back over to native or treed habitat is about a doubling of the soil holding capacity for rainfall, lessening of drying winds and an increase in overall fertility and therefore profitability of the land with better retention rates for lambing and calving and larger and healthier crops etc."

So we shouldn't get our knickers into a twist about this issue of native and even indigenous native?

"No, no need to do that! Just use common sense, goodwill and a compassionate heart and you can't go wrong."

Native. Non-native. Everything is native to God.

Growing From Your Own Saved Seed

Can you also tell me is there a difference in planting in the garden for seed you have saved yourself to seed you have bought in factory-made packets?

"We find that the plants grown from factories have a little tiredness about them. They are slower to germinate and have not the familiarity that a baby seed straight from a parent plant planted in a neighbouring region has. Saved seeds have more vitality, are stronger a better germination rates and have fewer pest and disease problems due to their innate intelligence about the region that they were born in. Their parent plants and the soil and skies and their fairy attendants attested to that. They pass on this intelligence. Then if this seed is carted away for miles and miles and grown in a completely different geographic region, they are at a loss as to where they have been taken to and where their land has gone? They have to start from scratch to build up their own information and intelligence about this new region. They also don't have the benefits of growing near sister and parent plants and the fairies that they are familiar with energetically. This gives them a noticeable disadvantage. This is why your own seed grown and collected from your own garden is the most viable and best closely followed by growing seed from neighbours and friends, local gardens and so forth.

'It takes a few generations for a plant and its seed, particularly with annuals to get used to an unfamiliar area and to perform at their best in them.'

'The other factor is that if you grow a garden that you lovingly tend and then collect this seed in love and delight, when you plant it back into your garden or give it away to someone, this love helps them perform much better than anything that was grown, harvested and packed by uncaring machines. Do you see?"

Yes, I do that is quite enlightening. I have always marveled at how much better one's own collected seed grows and germinates compared to bought packet seed, now I know why. I thought the packet seeds were just old.

"Yes, there is also that factor plus the chemicals in the packaging process too that hinder the growth process. You may eventually grow the said plants but at what cost to its future health and the health of the people eating it in the case of vegetable plants grown from factory seed."

Chapter 21
The Circle of Love

Everything is love. The circle is complete.

Gum trees do plants that we plant with our own hands and then care for and tend to them, do they go on to serve us?

"Yes, indeed these trees and plants have then been programmed so-to-speak into serving you and mainly you, they can of course serve others but their main aim will be to make your life better in any way they can."

What about trees from gardens that we have since left?

"They still remember you, and hope the day will come when you will visit them again. They still know what you are up to. In a sense they are like your loving children. But they can adjust to new hands if they tend them with love. These plants will in return shower the new occupants with loving care and attention."

So the act of love that we put into plants a plants and a whole garden that is returned to us manyfold?

"Yes indeed. This love forms a circle of love that keeps on going around and around. It touches whoever comes to the garden in a positive way. Plants that are planted with love are a blessing that keep on giving its gifts for eternity, or at least until that plant passes away and then even then that love energy still blesses the area. The energy of love is eternal."

'The energy of love is eternal' – the gum trees.

Can we 'retro-love' a garden or an area of natural vegetation?

"Yes, indeed you can add your love to already existing plants in an area in nature to increase the intensity of the love and healing that they have for you. It is simply a matter of degrees the highest and best form of protection is to surround yourself with plants that you have lovingly planted yourself."

So my garden that I have planted and tended for all these years is it an active circle of love for me and my family?

"Yes, indeed that is why you feel so happy and joyful out in it and how if you feel a little off, you feel immediately better when you go and sit out in it. Even if it is only sitting out on your front veranda. Verandas and balconies can also be very practical and healing indoor/outdoor spaces and should be used by humans more. To spend a lot more of their spare time in them even if it is to do a crossword or to have a cup of tea."

How long does it take to set up a garden with a circle of protective love?

"How long does it take to plant a shrub or to put a seed in the ground or to tend or appreciate a tree? That is all that is needed in the beginning stages to get the ball rolling. The effects are almost immediate. You will know that it is starting to work by the good feeling you get as you enter your new garden. This is not chance this is all your new plants beaming love back to you and it is a palpable feeling."

Great that's good news. I'll have to pay more attention when I next step out into my garden. It does feel good, but now I know why, I'll pay even more attention.

Heaven on Earth

I thought this was going to be a quiet unassuming little book on talking to the flora, but it has become so much more. I have learned so many loving ideas and tips for living an enhanced nature-based life. I am going to go out into my garden to try out some of the fairies' own ideas in the adventure that is my garden.

My gardening year is back to the place where it started. It has indeed been a year of talking to plants. Thanks to this book I have had the impetus and inclination to ask the plants and the fairies questions that I otherwise would not have thought to ask and probably would not have remembered if I hadn't recorded it on these pages.

I have gained a lot of knowledge and confidence in my abilities to accurately access telepathic information from the plants and even more amazingly, their fairy friends. So many of the things they talked about came to pass or could be verified one way or the other that I have no doubt of the veracity of the information.

Even though this book has come to an end, I feel like my adventures with plants and their attendant fairies are only just beginning. I am only really at the very beginning of interspecies communication and what is possible with these two-way conversations between fairy and human being. Think of all the lovely possibilities now that we know that interspecies communication is indeed conceivable?

Heaven on earth is a contradiction in terms, earth is heaven and heaven is earth.

Gardening and working in nature no longer has to be a matter of guesswork and chance. We just need to start co-creating with God, communicating with and acknowledging the consciousness and splendour all around us. We are indeed capable of knowing more about all the factors that affect our gardens and streetscapes, farms and forests. This is an opportunity to move to even greater heights, with man-plant communication we can move deep into the heart and soul of nature, taking us ever closer to living a life of heaven on earth.

In the heart of nature is the heart of God

Now it is up to you. Go outside, grab a trowel, laugh with a lily, converse with a conifer, it's time to start your own adventure! You may like to go out and talk with your own plants and see what happens or just rest assured, knowing that your plants are indeed conscious and consider you a part of their greater beloved family. Venture forth into nature and feel the love, it always has for you. Create your own garden with love. See the Universe in a flower and sense heaven in its perfume.

There is a fairy at the bottom of the garden, and it wants to be your friend.

Your garden knows you and loves you so.

More Books by the Author
Fairy Sparkles
Conversations With My Vegetable Garden

Sarah Rajkotwala Writer Social Media Links

My website : https://petalsandbuds.wordpress.com/[1]

My Blog : https://rosegardenconversation.wordpress.com/[2]

Instagram :
https://www.instagram.com/sarahrajkotwala_writer/[3]

1. https://l.facebook.com/
l.php?u=https%3A%2F%2Fpetalsandbuds.wordpress.com%2F%3Ffbclid%3DIwAR39t1or47bA1g2ggtvUkZf1BXSrRpnRssAul
9KPwTlxWbUTlGCaYwuBNos&h=AT3B1pP366gm_ukY5ONptP2sFwhPKLKd4yMhli8b7H_MnhYFYiHFePAO-
savS1_edp47RAfajxlN-e2lZUEHx-b47sM8qS_-x4v1BL4JXvFZsUqa-EmOg3Ev78oPPC793GMlXnyJaQ

2. https://rosegardenconversation.wordpress.com/?fbclid=IwAR3v3T4iZg4iNsdMWK1_PFV3MQ65rgJEphSibyXnkhH2iJQEK
s9x75n878w

3.   https://www.instagram.com/
sarahrajkotwala_writer/?fbclid=IwAR0M3z2Vxgv9MOcgDOhkRPeVYJ6orZEujsfpNjPeZLkpb34GVpr7SLg46Xg

SARAH RAJKOTWALA

About The Author

After many years of working in her own plant nursery Sarah Rajkotwala
realized she could talk to the plants and they could talk back!
She lives with her family and pets in a large rambling organic garden in
country South Australia, where she teaches fairy workshops and spiritual
development classes.

Don't miss out!

Visit the website below and you can sign up to receive emails whenever Sarah Rajkotwala publishes a new book. There's no charge and no obligation.

https://books2read.com/r/B-A-LGGK-GTJEB

BOOKS 2 READ

Connecting independent readers to independent writers.

Ingram Content Group UK Ltd.
Milton Keynes UK
UKHW020627200723
425492UK00016B/691